PADRE PIO

Colm Keane has published 16 books, including bestsellers *Nervous Breakdown*, *Death and Dying*, *The Stress File*, *The Teenage Years* and *The Jobs Crisis*. He is a graduate of Trinity College, Dublin, and Georgetown University, Washington DC. As a broadcaster, he won a Jacob's Award and a Glaxo Fellowship for European Science Writers. His most recent publications are *Hurling's Top 20*, *Gaelic Football's Top 20* and *Ireland's Soccer Top 20*.

Colm Keane

PADRE PIO
The Irish Connection

MAINSTREAM
PUBLISHING

EDINBURGH AND LONDON

First published in Great Britain in 2007 by
MAINSTREAM PUBLISHING COMPANY
(EDINBURGH) LTD
7 Albany Street
Edinburgh EH1 3UG

ISBN 9781845962852

Photograph of Padre Pio, p. 8, courtesy of
Edizione Voce di Padre Pio

A catalogue record for this book is available
from the British Library

Typeset in Sabon and Trajan

Printed in Great Britain by
Clays Ltd, St Ives plc

FOR SEÁN

CONTENTS

INTRODUCTION

ASK ANY DEVOTEE OF PADRE PIO HOW THEIR adoration began and you are guaranteed an interesting story. They will, almost certainly, recount some personal or family crisis, recovery from illness, relief from suffering, or receipt of a special favour or grace. Invariably, their existence has been transformed by blessings so meaningful that a lifetime of veneration ensues. What's more, the favours are reciprocated with a sense of intense gratitude and unwavering appreciation that is rare to encounter.

Throughout cities, towns, villages and townlands in Ireland, there's a thriving devotion to Padre Pio. It quietly goes about its business, occasionally raising its head in parish newsletters or community notes announcing prayer meetings or signalling the arrival of a mitten or glove. Beyond that, this circle of adoration courts no publicity or seeks no acclaim. Its activities are virtually ignored, almost never covered on radio or television and seldom referred to by the press. Although always in motion, it's as if this vast network of Padre Pio devotion doesn't exist.

Not a week goes by without thousands of devotees quietly gathering in the name of Padre Pio. They meet in tiny chapels, community halls, living rooms or kitchens, their cars jammed into overfull car parks and their venues 'standing room only'. They pray together for their own intentions or for the intentions of others. Never promoting themselves or pushing their stories, they reluctantly discuss their devotion in the interests of repaying favours or providing inspiration to those who are in need. It's a remarkable phenomenon; a low, throbbing undercurrent of religious fervour, far removed from Bible-thumping fundamentalism yet with its own vibrant intensity.

At the centre of this devotion is a man who, since the end of the First World War, has touched and transformed countless lives. Born in 1887, Francesco Forgione grew up in poverty-stricken circumstances in the village of Pietrelcina, which is located about 40 miles from the Italian city of Naples. His parents, with their tiny farm, struggled to provide for their family's needs. One thing that didn't cost money was faith and there was an abundance of that. As a boy who conversed with Jesus and Our Lady, Francesco was regarded as blessed and holy. Drawn to the spiritual life, he decided at the age of 14 to pursue a religious vocation and did so in 1903 when he embarked on becoming a Capuchin friar.

Taking the name of Pio, which translates as 'Pius', Padre Pio developed a reputation for intense devotion and fervent prayer. At the age of 29 he first took up residence at the friary of Our Lady of Grace at San Giovanni Rotondo. There, his mystical qualities drew crowds to Confession and attracted the first of his committed devotees. Two years after his arrival, in 1918, a most extraordinary, supernatural occurrence took place. It involved the appearance on his body of the stigmata of Jesus: the wounds of the crucifixion that appeared on his hands, feet and side, which he would painfully bear for the next 50 years of his life. He was aged 31 at the time.

Within months word spread of this remarkable friar who was touched by sanctity. Locals, especially devout women, were drawn by his presence. The first visitors arrived to attend Confession and to seek blessings. In the early 1920s news radiated even further, helped by extensive press coverage. He was soon known throughout Italy. The response of the secular clergy was swift and vicious. Jealous of his fame and the crowds he attracted, they made stinging accusations to the authorities in Rome.

Alleging that he lingered in the company of women, wore perfume and make-up, conducted improper Confessions and effectively fostered a money-making racket at San Giovanni, his reputation was torn to pieces. He was, as a result, banned from saying public Masses, hearing lay Confessions, meeting with devotees, answering letters or revealing his stigmata in public. Cut off from his spiritual children, he prayed, said Mass in private and lived the life of a simple priest. His pastoral duties removed, he was effectively a prisoner in the friary at San Giovanni.

Restored to his public ministry at the age of 46, Padre Pio quickly became known for his charismatic gifts and mysterious powers. The lame cast off their crutches and walked. The blind recovered their sight. Tumours disappeared from those with cancer. Strange, sweet perfumes emanated from the blood of his wounds. He appeared at the bedsides of the sick in their homes while simultaneously being witnessed by his colleagues back at the friary. Those attending his Confessions were shocked when he read their souls, recounting sins only they could have known. Disbelievers were converted. The wayward returned to their faith.

The dusty road leading to the friary of Our Lady of Grace was soon filled with the sick and unwell, penitents, the curious; the poor, rich and famous all seeking time with this living saint. Sacks of letters arrived each week asking for miracles, prayers or spiritual advice. Italian Prime Minister Aldo Moro, King Alfonso of Spain and Spanish dictator Francisco Franco either sought his counsel or came to visit. Songwriter Irving Berlin and opera star Beniamino Gigli also made their way up the dirt track to the friary. Crowning it all, each day came hundreds of fanatical women, many from the town of San Giovanni, waiting at the door of the chapel for Mass or anticipating his arrival at Confession.

Among those to visit in the 1940s was the young Karol Wojtyla, later to become Pope John Paul II. Calling on Padre Pio as a young priest, it appears that he asked him to hear his Confession. While Vicar Capitular of Krakow in Poland, he also requested Padre Pio to pray for a friend with cancer who was facing a serious operation. Shortly prior to surgery it was discovered that the cancer had disappeared. No operation was necessary. No doubt impressed by the miracle, Karol Wojtyla, as Pope, fast-tracked Padre Pio's beatification and canonisation. In doing so, he created a lasting connection between these two most popular of churchmen who, to this day, remain at the forefront of public affection.

Perhaps the greatest of Padre Pio's earthly miracles was the founding of the internationally renowned hospital Casa Sollievo della Sofferenza, or the Home for the Relief of Suffering, at San Giovanni Rotondo. Although a long-held dream of Padre Pio's, the aspiration of building and running a modern hospital in the remote Gargano Mountains was greeted with similar scepticism as the subsequent construction of an international airport at Knock. Contributing the first donation to the hospital building fund, which he had received as an offering, Padre Pio's plans were initially put into motion in 1940. Interrupted by the war, work began in earnest in 1947. Opening in 1956, the Casa went on to become one of the most impressive hospitals in Europe.

By the 1960s Padre Pio was ageing fast. His body was crippled with the pain and discomfort of his wounds. He could barely walk due to the swelling of his feet. Suffering from sleep deprivation, breathlessness and fatigue, he continued to attend to his priestly ministry, rising early in the morning, saying Mass and hearing Confessions. How he continued to perform these functions after so many decades of suffering is anyone's guess. Persecution was never far away, with further investigations of his personal popularity and alleged financial mismanagement of the hospital dogging him into his later years.

Throughout 1967 Padre Pio's health faded rapidly. Already, mysteriously, the signs of the stigmata were disappearing. The wounds diminished and then departed from his feet. The wound on his side was next. Finally, in early 1968 the wounds on his hands started to vanish and by summer only dry crusts and a pink redness were discernible. In retrospect, it must have been obvious that his earthly mission was coming to a close.

Padre Pio's death finally arrived on 23 September 1968, just days after the fiftieth anniversary of receiving the visible stigmata and with San Giovanni packed with an assembly of prayer groups. Aged 81, he was, at the end, tired and feeble, in pain and certainly aware of his pending departure. To the last, he was, as he called himself, 'only a poor friar who prays', his final invocation being the simplest of all, 'Jesus . . . Mary . . . Jesus . . . Mary.'

There are many people to be thanked for their help with this book. I am grateful, in particular, to that small group of Irish men and women who are still with us and who met Padre Pio or attended his Mass and Confession at San Giovanni Rotondo. Tom Cooney, Donald Enright, Mona Hanafin, Father Pius McLaughlin OFM, Catherine Maguire, Margot Scannell and Kay Thornton are among those who provided me with living testimony. Kathleen O'Sullivan sent letters to Padre Pio, while Mary Briody, Patricia Connolly, Rosalyn O'Mahoney and Stella Enright contributed information about contacts established by deceased members of their families.

Thanks to all who spoke about the miracles, graces and blessings either they or others have received. All were generous with their time and pleasant to deal with, including Arthur Beales, Nuala Brady, Maureen Broderick, Brendan Byrne, Nora Cantillon, Father Gerard Coleman, Patricia Comiskey, Kathleen Connolly, Liam Coyle, Amanda Coyne, Lucy Cranney, Kitty Cullen, John Cunningham, Ellen C. from Cork, Alice de la Cour, Gemma Dillon, Mary Duff, Father Michael Duggan, Marie Durack, Madeleine Forkan, Noreen Handley, Kay Harrington, Chris Hayes, Betty Hennessy and Joseph Lacey.

My gratitude to Father Jack Mc Ardle ss.cc., Brigid McCaffrey, Margaret McDonagh, Hubert Mc Hugh, Josephine Mc Laughlin, Eileen Maguire, Mary from County Waterford, Betty Moran, Tom Mulligan, Sean Mulrine, Cáit Murray, Elisa Muscedere, Tom Neary, Niamh from County Kerry, Assumpta O'Brien, Eileen O'Donnell, Pauline from County Clare, Angelo Perma, Alex Quinn, Eileen Rea, Rita who once lived in County Cork, Rose from County Kerry, Marian Sheedy, Jane Smyth, Nancy Surlis and Marie Toone. My appreciation also to Sammy Revins Junior for permission to use his late father's interview broadcast on Community Radio Youghal.

Thanks to Ned Keane, Marie Keane and Pat Kennedy from County Waterford. I am likewise indebted to Pat Devlin, Chrissie White and Oliver Mc Garvey from Bray, County Wicklow. Mary Gannon and Father Joseph Gavigan, County Mayo, were always uplifting, as were Garry Sullivan, Peter Carr, Fionnuala Hayes and Kathleen O'Connor. Also gracious with their time were Maureen, Marie and Dolores at the Padre Pio office in Dublin, where Eileen Maguire was an enormous encouragement and a font of wisdom. Once again, the publishers Mainstream were a pleasure to work with, in particular Bill Campbell, Peter MacKenzie, Graeme Blaikie and Ailsa Bathgate. Lee Fullarton deserves special praise for her creativity and perseverance in designing the cover. My appreciation also to Lorraine McCann.

No one was a truer inspiration than William 'Nooche' Kenefick from Youghal, County Cork, who provided sterling help throughout this project. His priceless advice, encouragement and ideas were always just a phone call away. Thanks to his wife Agnes for her patience and insightful remarks. So many others also had suggestions regarding people to interview. One source from Munster, who wishes to remain anonymous, was a true guardian angel. He steered me in the right direction, encouraged me when spirits were flagging and identified people willing to talk. His assistance was invaluable.

This project could not have been completed without the support of Seán Keane and Úna O'Hagan. It was Seán who inspired the book. His star shone brightly during times often clouded by darkness. Úna read the text and steered me in the right direction. Father Ermelindo, who heads up the English office at San Giovanni Rotondo, and Julie Kerry Cifaldi, who works with *The Voice of Padre Pio,* were ever helpful. Nor can I forget the Immaculate Sisters of Saint Clare in San Giovanni, especially Sister Ofelia, and the Carmelite Sisters in Malahide, County Dublin.

Finally, my thanks to Padre Pio whose hand guided the research and compilation work behind this book. The coincidences and fortuitous happenings encountered during this project convince me that he was never far away. Mislaid telephone numbers mysteriously resurfaced, people who were hard to find suddenly became contactable, documents were effortlessly rediscovered, avenues of investigation opened up with uncanny ease. When things flagged, invariably the phone rang and I was off again. Never has a text been easier to put together. But why should I be surprised? As the following chapters reveal, his are strange and wonderful ways; mystical, supernatural, miraculous, all the while directing us and illuminating the path ahead. It's to his powerful legacy that this book is ultimately dedicated.

Colm Keane
August 2007

EARLY DEVOTION

To the Irish setting out for San Giovanni Rotondo in the 1950s, it must have felt like the ultimate pilgrimage. They first travelled long journeys by air in old prop planes. They then wound their way by slow trains and battered old buses as they climbed into the remote and inhospitable Gargano Mountains in the spur of Italy. Walking up the final stretch of dirt track, tired and hungry, they arrived at the isolated sixteenth-century friary of Our Lady of Grace on the outskirts of San Giovanni Rotondo. In residence was a living saint bearing the wounds of Christ, whose intense holiness had been brought to the attention of an incredulous world.

It was certainly like no other journey these Irish pilgrims had undertaken before. What took them so long was the sheer magnitude of the trip. In those days Italy seemed a world away, cut off not only by distance but by the high costs of travel. Ireland was a tiny, isolated island trapped by poverty and suffocated by a multitude of physical and social restrictions. Outings to Lough Derg and Knock were the height of it. Occasional trips to Lourdes or Fatima were only for the highly committed. But religious conviction was a compelling force. Grounded in the intense Irish Catholicism of the 1950s, for some the search for spiritual meaning was boundless.

By the time they first arrived in Italy in the 1950s, Padre Pio was ageing fast. As the decade came to a close, he was in his 70s. Rapidly, however, industrialisation took off in Ireland and economic buoyancy ensued. Prosperity was everywhere. Suddenly, people had money. Group travel expanded. Package tours came into vogue. No longer did far-flung hills, like those surrounding San Giovanni, seem quite so far away. Inevitably, the trickle of pilgrims became a flow.

Joining the long queue of world visitors were hundreds, and soon thousands, of Irish people, many of them women. Those who couldn't travel wrote instead. Letters winged their way from all counties of Ireland to San Giovanni. Somehow, they all seemed inexorably drawn to this mystical mountain outcrop where a strange Capuchin friar was residing. They believed him to be a saint. Time would prove them right.

KAY THORNTON, COUNTY DUBLIN, DESCRIBES HER PIONEERING VISIT TO PADRE PIO IN THE 1950s.
In 1955 my sister Emer and I went out to meet Padre Pio, never having been away before. We had read a book on him by Charles Mortimer Carty. My sister had picked it up in my aunt's house and it was lying around at home. We were immediately drawn to him. He has this way of drawing you. We knew nothing about travelling. We were very green and were just like children. It was a very difficult trip in those days. We prayed to Padre Pio, 'Look, Padre Pio, you know we are coming and you will have to look after us.'

Everything that happened was unbelievable. The people in Rome thought we were crazy, they didn't know anything about Padre Pio. When we were on the train from Rome, a young man happened to come into the carriage. He was Italian but he spoke perfect English. We were talking about Padre Pio and we told him we were going to San Giovanni. He said, 'You are on the wrong train.' It's hard to believe but he turned out to be a spiritual child of Padre Pio. He directed us and we arrived there safely.

San Giovanni was very primitive at the time. I was very nervous and terrified of being so far away from home. It was a different era. We went to Padre Pio's Mass. We were up at the door at about half past four in the morning. The people were there in their black shawls. They were very rude to us and they just elbowed us out of the way. We were so simple; we didn't know what they were doing. They resented us. Anyway, we got in and we were right opposite the altar in the little chapel. I remember him trembling after the Consecration. He literally trembled. It has stuck in my mind.

Later on, we wanted to know how to meet him. We went to the office and I said to the man, 'We want to see Padre Pio. How can we do it?' He didn't speak any English but he went off and he got this American friar. He gave us two little pieces of paper, like tickets, and he said for us to come back at a certain time when Padre Pio would be passing through a corridor. He said, 'You will see him then.'

We were right beside him when he walked by. He was dressed in the ordinary brown habit with a white cord. He had this strange effect on you. We weren't able to speak. He had the same effect on a lot of people. He was a big man and he had the most fantastic eyes. I just wanted to touch him. So I touched him and he sprung around. I thought he was going to give out to me. But he never said a word. He looked straight into my eyes.

I felt that he could see directly into my soul. I felt that he knew everything. His eyes were marvellous. They were big, brown eyes and they looked straight into you. There was no wavering. And that was that. Our trip was so unusual that there was a piece in the paper afterwards to say that two sisters had gone out to Italy to see this man. It was big news.

THE LATE MAIREAD DOYLE WAS ANOTHER PIONEERING TRAVELLER TO SAN GIOVANNI, ACCORDING TO HER NIECE MARY BRIODY, COUNTY WESTMEATH. MAIREAD SUBSEQUENTLY FOUNDED IRELAND'S FIRST PADRE PIO PRAYER GROUP, WHICH WAS LOCATED IN DUBLIN.

Mairead was coming home on a bus one evening in the 1950s and she found a book about Padre Pio, written by a priest. She decided, 'I must go and see this man.' She made the trek on her own, there was no such thing as organised tours at that stage. She flew to London and then to Rome. She then got a train and a bus and walked up the last bit. It was a terrible old trek, especially on your own. It was a huge ordeal just to go. Later, they said she was the first Irish girl to come up the dirt track to San Giovanni back in the 1950s.

His Mass was on at five o'clock in the morning. She was first outside the door but when she got in she was last because the Italians just pushed her out of the way. The second morning they didn't push her because she had learnt. She made herself known and then she got an audience. She was that type of woman who would make herself known, she wouldn't just walk away. So she got in to see Padre Pio.

She was very taken with his spirituality. She said you couldn't take your eyes off the altar during Mass. She said that his eyes seemed to penetrate through you. She was afraid of flying and he told her that he'd always accompany her on a plane journey. She wrote to him regularly and sent him telegrams. They were about any little thing going on in her life. It wouldn't have to be a major thing. He'd write back to her.

She went over every year. She brought every one of us over too. When her parents died Mairead went in and asked him, 'Are they in heaven?' He said, 'No, they still need more prayer.' So she got loads of Masses said. The next year she went, he said, 'Your mamma's soul is in heaven.' Then, when my father went he was part of the last Irish group to be with Padre Pio just before he died. She arranged an audience. My father went in. Padre Pio blessed everyone and then he came back to my father and blessed him again. He must have known something because my father died a few months later.

MARGOT SCANNELL, CORK, ENCOUNTERED PADRE PIO ON FOUR OCCASIONS IN THE 1950S AND '60S.

In 1956 I was taken very ill and I had a complete hysterectomy at the age of 27. A book about Padre Pio was handed in to the hospital but I hadn't time to read it until after my operation. In the meantime I decided to go to Italy. The reason I made the decision was because on my way to theatre I saw this statue of St Philomena. I looked up at the statue and said, 'If I come out of this I will go to you in thanksgiving.'

My husband, John, was a CIE clerk. He had free travel and I had half travel. We went by boat and overland: Cork to Dun Laoghaire, Holyhead, London, Dover, Calais, then through France and on to Rome. It took us three days to get there and three days to get back. From Rome we went beyond Naples to St Philomena's shrine. The next day, after seeing the shrine, we were due to go to the Isle of Capri but some people from Waterford said, 'We are not going with you, we are going to a stigmatist.' I said, 'What stigmatist?' They said, 'Padre Pio.' 'Oh,' I said, 'we'll go, I read all about him.'

I saw him that first time I went. He was hearing the women's Confessions. He never had the curtains closed. The curtains would be open and you could see him. He would be looking out as well as hearing Confessions. I was in the crowd. The woman from Waterford kept saying, 'Do you feel his eyes on you? Do you feel his eyes going through you?' I felt I did, that his eyes were going right through me. Next thing, his eyes moved and they fixed on a woman near me. He called her out of the crowd and brought her up to the Confession box. When that woman went up he pulled both curtains over. When the Confession was over you could see the affection in the woman. She was crying. It was unbelievable.

A few years later we went out again and that time I saw him passing through a room. I remember saying a prayer before he came in, 'Lord, I am not worthy that thou should enter under my roof. Only say the word and my soul shall be healed.' Before he even came through the door there was a smell of ointment which went all over me. I will never forget it. I felt it was the cleaning of my soul.

I then met him a third time, in the mid-1960s. Father Joseph, who helped look after Padre Pio and who I got to know, sent word down to the dining-room of the hotel to say that I was wanted above. I was staying in the Santa Maria delle Grazie, which was the only hotel at the time. When I went up he said, 'I'll get you into this room and Padre Pio will meet you.' He came into the room we were in. God help him, if you saw him trying to walk, he was shuffling along and his feet were all swollen. The priests were holding him up under his arms. He looked like a lovely old priest.

There were only about six or eight women there. He started with the first person and Father Joseph introduced her. He looked right through her, nothing happened between them. It came to my turn and Father Joseph introduced me. He looked right through me and never spoke either. But he put out his hand for me to kiss and then continued on. Eventually, he came to this Italian lady and he got very cross. Afterwards, I said to Father Joseph, 'What happened?' He said, 'She was trying to fool him.' He said that Padre Pio said that why he had to speak crossly to her was because God was ready to strike her.

The final time I met him was in 1968, a fortnight before he died. Father Joseph again got us to see him. That time I met him on the way down to the crypt. Father Joseph said, 'Padre Pio said that when he comes out you are not to speak with your lips, you are to speak with your heart and he will know what you want.' He went in for him and brought him out to the landing where you go down to the crypt. He was in a wheelchair. He looked very frail.

He looked right through each person while they asked in their hearts what they wanted. When he had looked at every one of us, he told a priest to take his chair around and he put out his hand for us to kiss. Some he didn't touch, I'd say because they didn't need it. But I needed it. He put out his hand for me to kiss but I couldn't get at it. Instead, he gave me a fine slap down on the head. Afterwards, I said to Father Joseph, 'What did that mean?' He said, 'What you asked for, he was giving you his protection.'

It was great to have met him. I loved him but was afraid of him at the same time because he could read every bit of you. It was wonderful to be in his presence. He was sad to look at. You knew he was suffering. You were looking at a suffering man. You could see him shuffling along. Even when he was in his chair you felt he was suffering. To be honest with you, I felt that God was there, I felt it was God.

DONALD ENRIGHT, COUNTY CORK, RECALLS HIS FIRST MEETING WITH PADRE PIO.

Back in 1959 my mother suffered from incurable cancer. She was in her 50s. She had womb cancer and it had spread into the rectum. I took a book out of the library about Padre Pio and I decided to write to him. I asked him for a cure for my mother and, if not, that she would die without knowing she was dying and die without pain. He wrote back telling me to have confidence in God and that I would get my intentions.

One evening my mother said to me that she would have to have an operation and she was going to talk to the surgeon about it. I knew that he would tell her that an operation wasn't possible. I was desperate and very worried. But that night she got a clot between the lung and the heart. The doctors dissolved it. She got a second clot. I was sent for and she died the following morning at half past two. She died in my arms.

So she never knew. It was exactly the same death that Padre Pio had in 1968 when he died from a clot between the lung and the heart at half past two in the morning and died in a priest's arms.

A year later I went to San Giovanni. I had by then been in contact with Father Eusebio, who was Padre Pio's secretary for the English language. He wanted me to meet Padre Pio. I arrived on 5 October and my mother's anniversary was on 6 October. When I was due to meet Padre Pio I ran out of the church. I felt I wasn't worthy to meet him. I went to Confession and the next day I met him.

Immediately Padre Pio saw me he said, 'My son, you did not come here to save your mother's soul. Your mother who is in heaven and I brought you here to meet me.' I couldn't credit what I was listening to. He had no idea of who I was and had never seen me before in my life. I was mesmerised. I felt overwhelmed, overjoyed. I kissed his hand and he saw the tears of emotion in my eyes. He just looked at me and he walked away. I will never forget it.

I met him on many occasions after that. He was approximately 5 ft 11 in. He had large, dark-brown eyes. He dressed in the brown Capuchin habit and his sandals were very large on account of the wounded feet. He wore white socks by night and brown socks by day so that people wouldn't see the blood on the white. He had a look of love on his face most of the time. Yet he could also be very frank. I felt totally unworthy to stand in his presence. There was an aura of saintliness about him. I realised I was in the presence of a saint who was suffering so much for others.

He was capable of humour. One day, while looking out through the window of the church, he cried when he saw all the people coming up. He said, 'I don't know why they are coming here to meet me.' Father Eusebio said in an attempt to lift him up, 'I'm sorry, Father, but they are coming to meet me.' He laughed then. Another time a priest came with a group of people. He was an Italian and the Italians are often long-winded in their homilies. After Mass was over he met with Padre Pio. He said to Padre Pio, 'What did you think of my homily today?' Padre Pio said, 'Good, but if you kept on much longer you'd be talking to yourself.' His sense of humour came through all the time.

Another time I was with Father Eusebio when Padre Pio arrived into our company. Father Eusebio said to Padre Pio, 'This is my most beloved friend from Ireland, kiss his hand.' He was being humorous. I was shocked to think of him going to kiss my hand. Instead, he gave me his hand to kiss. When I looked up I saw his eyes. He had large brown eyes. But they had changed from brown to a golden colour and they were spinning in his head. He gave me three taps on my forehead. His eyes were still golden and spinning in his head. He was reading the state of my soul. He had that gift.

MONA HANAFIN, COUNTY TIPPERARY, CREDITS A VISIT TO PADRE PIO WITH HER MIRACULOUS CURE FROM CANCER.

In 1963 I went to San Giovanni for the first time. The following year I was very, very ill with cancer. I was in my mid-20s. I was in and out of hospital and I wasn't getting any better. I lost an awful lot of weight and eventually the doctor said to me that he would have to remove the womb altogether and it would have to be done immediately.

I said to him, 'I'm going to Padre Pio and he will cure me.' I left all my tablets at home and my mother and I went off to see Padre Pio. I was very ill on the streets in Rome. I had been very ill like that all the time, with constant vomiting and the likes. When I went down to San Giovanni, the Mass was at five o'clock in the morning. My poor mother read the clock upside down and she had me up at twenty to two.

We waited at the doors of the church until they opened at about a quarter to five. Then there was a rush in the door. The

Italian people thought he was their own. During the winter they had him to themselves, there was nobody else around. Here was my mother and I coming in and taking their places. They were very protective of him, and rightly so.

We decided that I had to get near Padre Pio. We got into the church within two pews of where he was so I saw him very, very clearly during the Mass. I saw the stigmata when he removed the glove during the Consecration; that's the only time he removed the glove. He turned around and he blessed everybody. I was with a group of other people and when I came out I said, 'Padre Pio was looking straight at me.' They said, 'No, he was looking straight at us.' In one glance he encompassed the whole church.

We had Mass at five o'clock every morning. He said the Angelus at twelve o'clock from the gallery in the old church where he got the stigmata, where we joined him in prayer. In the afternoons he would pray up in the gallery of the new church. We'd all go and pray downstairs and be looking up at him. At night-time we all went around to the side to say goodnight to him. He had a handkerchief which he would wave and we'd wave handkerchiefs back.

I was still very ill and our group had an audience with him in the old church. When we came in, we came from the sunshine into the darkness and we couldn't see down to the Confessional until our eyes were adjusted. We were all wondering where Padre Pio was. I looked down and, as the Confessional was open to view, the next thing was that I saw him and he was looking up. I said to Mammy, 'He is looking up at me.'

We were all lined up on either side of the pews and I was at the altar rails. Padre Pio was going to pass up through us all. The custom was that he would give you his hand and you would kiss it. That was the Italian custom. But I had read in a book that Padre Pio could see into your soul and I said, 'I don't believe I'll be good enough to do that.' I was looking at him and saying in my mind, 'If you think I'm good enough would you put your hand on my head and bless me?' He did. When he walked up and came to me he put his hand on my head and he blessed me.

I stayed in San Giovanni for about four days. I was very ill coming back on the plane and I was brought straight out to the hospital. Mammy said to the doctor, 'My daughter is not well at all.' He said, 'Get her checked into one of the hospitals in Dublin.' I went unconscious and I remained that way for two or three days or more. My temperature was 106.5. They gave me the last rites. I actually had gone so far that I could see myself from outside. I was looking down at myself and I could name who was around the bed.

They sent for my family and my husband. They said, 'She won't pull through.' But I did come through the following day. When I came to, the cancer was gone. That's over 40 years ago. I never got it back. I promised Padre Pio, in thanksgiving, that I would bring groups to San Giovanni. I have been doing so ever since 1968 and I continue to do so to this day.

Before I started taking groups, in the early days before the 1960s, there were very few people from Ireland going to San Giovanni. It was an awfully long trip and things weren't great in Ireland. Many went overland, it was horrendous. The furthest you'd go at the time was to England or Dublin. When you got there it wasn't like it is now. There was no big Way of the Cross like there is there now; there was only a small Way of the Cross on the road up. There were only one or two hotels.

Yet the Irish were some of the first to go there in large numbers in the 1960s. They had great faith. They had a great feeling for Padre Pio. Some had relations in Italy. The Irish also were used to pilgrimages; they would make pilgrimages to Croagh Patrick from Kerry or anywhere in Ireland. They were used to going to Knock. So it wasn't a hardship. Since then there's been a flood of people travelling to San Giovanni from Ireland.

PADRE PIO'S ROLE IN THE SCULPTING OF THE STATUE OF OUR LADY OF KNOCK, IN THE 1950s, IS RECOUNTED BY TOM NEARY, AUTHOR AND AUTHORITY ON KNOCK SHRINE.

In the 1950s it was decided to replace the statuary at the shrine in Knock. There was a woman in Knock at the time called Mrs Judy Coyne and she was asked to go to Rome to see could she find an artist who could make proper statuary and get it right in every detail. Mrs Coyne knew quite a lot of people in Rome, she had contacts, so she went there and through recommendations she found this brilliant artist, Professor Lorenzo Ferri. She went to him and explained her problem.

He then made models for her to see. She was fairly satisfied with some of them, for example the saints Joseph and John the Evangelist. They seemed to be reasonably good in her eyes. The other parts, like the altar and the lamb and the cross, weren't too difficult. But Our Lady didn't seem to be the way the witnesses had described her. She kept at him and at him and at him. She was a very particular woman, who wouldn't take a second-rate product. She had quite a time with him sorting the whole thing out.

The artist was very interested to get the face right. Because Christ didn't have an earthly father he held that there had to be a resemblance between the son and the mother. Therefore, he said that Mary would have features like her son. He also looked at the Shroud of Turin. He then based his work on those propositions. What he came up with then was Our Lady's face as it might have been in the apparition.

Mrs Coyne was not happy with this. It didn't seem to come up to her standards and they often fought in the workshop over it. He used to say, 'Mrs Coyne, you are looking for the divine but I can only give you the human, there's a limit to what I can do.' She said, 'I know what you're trying to do but it's not quite the way that it needs to be.'

What she wanted was something close to the description given by the principal witness at Knock, who had given a great description of Our Lady. The witness had explained how her hands were, how her face was, what she looked like, her colouring and that she didn't wear any shoes or sandals on her feet, you could see her feet and one foot was in advance of the other. She also described the positioning of her hands in relation to her shoulders, the crown on her head and the rose on her forehead. She always said that she was 'a real Jewess' and that she looked like a Jewish woman.

Unknown to the artist, Mrs Coyne went to San Giovanni. Padre Pio was alive at the time. She went to Padre Pio's Mass. During the Mass she made a request that the artist in Rome would be able to complete Our Lady's statue so that it would be right. The artist didn't know anything about this visit to San Giovanni. When Mrs Coyne came back to Rome she went down to the workshop. As she was coming towards the workshop she saw that he had placed all the statues outside. Immediately, she looked and she said, 'Oh, this is it.' She came closer and she said, 'That's exactly it.'

She went in to the artist. He was in poor enough health at that time in his life. She said, 'What has happened since I was in last?' He said, 'Well, I was in bed and I wasn't feeling well but I got this flash of inspiration. I jumped out of bed, I went down to the workshop and I worked furiously until my inspiration was in the statue.' She said, 'That's extraordinary, what day was that?' The interesting thing was that the actual inspiration came to him at the exact time and day that Mrs Coyne was at Padre Pio's Mass in San Giovanni. He could not get the thing right until that particular day. And that's the statue that's there at Knock Shrine to this day.

GERRY FITZGERALD, A PADRE PIO DEVOTEE AND CAFÉ OWNER FROM LIMERICK, ORGANISED TOURS TO SAN GIOVANNI IN THE LATE 1950s BECOMING THE FIRST PERSON IN IRELAND TO DO SO. HIS ACHIEVEMENT IS REMEMBERED BY TOM COONEY, COUNTY CLARE.

Gerry Fitzgerald lived in Limerick, where he owned the Palm Grove Café in Upper Cecil Street. He was a fine, respectable-looking man. He was tall. He knew Padre Pio and he would talk about Padre Pio all the time. Every time we met he talked about him. In fact, there is a photograph of him sitting on a seat with Padre Pio standing over him. I used to go once a week to the café to meet him. We were personal friends and we used to be at Mass together in the Dominican church.

He was the only man around Clare, Tipperary, Limerick and Galway who was doing these trips and is believed to be the first in Ireland to do so. About 40 people would have gone with him. Many of them would have been afraid of flying at the time. They travelled by the old planes which were smaller and not able to take the crowds they can take now. Also, you would be travelling to San Giovanni from Rome on a coach. If you had over 40 people, or so, they wouldn't be able to be carried on the coach. You'd have to get another coach and that wouldn't pay.

He did seven tours, one after another. His last tour was in October 1965, which I went on. He got sick a short time after coming back. I used to call to see him. He died in 1966 and I was at his funeral. I think he was in his 60s when he died. His family were grown up, including a daughter who was a great painter. He always used to say that he was delighted he did seven trips, one year after the other. I then took over from him, if you like. I organised a few tours with his late wife and then I did them by myself from 1979 into the 1980s and 1990s.

NUALA BRADY, FORMER ITALIAN PILGRIMAGE MANAGER FOR JOE WALSH TOURS, REFLECTS ON THE EARLY TOURS TO SAN GIOVANNI.

There were a lot more groups going out in the early days. We had a direct flight into Bari Airport every week. People had great devotion to him at that time and they wanted to stay there for a week. Nowadays, nobody wants to go there for a week; they want to do Rome, Assisi and see more. Eventually, television brought these places into people's homes.

You didn't have the choice of hotels that you have now and the standard wouldn't have been as good. People seemed to take it as being a pilgrimage, in the real sense of the word. They didn't mind the inconvenience and putting up with it. Nowadays, it's totally different, they want their good hotels and there's too many of them down there now.

A lot of people who travelled in the old days would have been from the country and they were very comfortable with the old San Giovanni, which was old world. It felt like going to a little old country town. That was quite comfortable for a lot of people. But it has got very commercial now. It also was much more religious and there was a lot more praying. In those days they would probably have said the Rosary on the flight going over. The priest would have been allowed to speak on the microphone on the aircraft, which wouldn't be allowed at all now.

People saved for the trip as the big holiday of the year. It was dearer at the time, relatively speaking. It would have cost them much more then than it costs today, and they are more affluent now. Lots of prayer groups would go. They would arrange these trips away and the over 55s and over 65s would put money into an account every week, or every few weeks, and build it up over the year. They would plan it all year round. In some ways they may have appreciated it more because it took more effort.

CATHERINE MAGUIRE, COUNTY CAVAN, TRAVELLED WITH A
TOUR IN 1962.

I first went in September 1962. I had read a book about Padre
Pio and I wanted the privilege to be there at his Mass. Joe
Walsh ran that tour. I think it cost about £100, not much over
it anyway. It was an awful lot of money because salaries were
so small at the time. We flew by propeller plane, a Viscount I
think it was. We shared the plane with other passengers who
were only going to Rome. It was a long trip. We flew from
Dublin to Brussels and then to Rome. We had to stop off in
Brussels, I believe. We came down for refuelling.

It was the first time they took people there by bus from
Rome. They always went by train previous to that. The bus
driver, who was Italian, lost his way. There were about 30
or 40 of us on the bus. He hadn't an idea where we were.
We were lost up the mountains and it was two o'clock in
the morning before we arrived. He got into a lot of trouble
getting us there although he was alright coming back.

Italy was very poor then. It wasn't that long after the war; it
was ravaged. There weren't so many houses or hotels around.
Nobody could speak English; now quite a number can. We
stayed in the only hotel there at the time. Things were pretty
primitive. The place was very nice but the food wasn't the
best. The food was so different. We wouldn't even have seen
spaghetti in Ireland back in those days. But it was the end of
September and the weather was beautiful.

I went to his five o'clock Mass in the mornings. I went every
day. The Mass was something else. The crowds were huge.
The villagers were there from about two o'clock or three
o'clock in the morning, standing outside to get in. I was there
from about a half an hour beforehand. He was so prayerful at
the Mass, it was lovely.

It was very hard to meet him even then. The natives
wouldn't like you getting close to him. He called round one
day to see us. He came in and blessed us in a little place near

the convent. We all knelt down. He was very frail at that time. He had the wounds and there was somebody always helping him around. Unfortunately, the natives were banging on the door and created an awful fuss. They didn't want outsiders to be there at all. I didn't want to be fussing to get over near to him. Anyway, he didn't stay long.

I spent five days in San Giovanni, I think, on that first trip. It was a long time but San Giovanni was nicer and certainly a more real place at that time. We came back via Rome. I then went every year in the 1960s except for the year he died. I was devoted to him then all my life.

TOM COONEY, COUNTY CLARE, MET PADRE PIO DURING HIS PILGRIMAGE IN 1965.

I happened to go to San Giovanni three years before Padre Pio died. I was one of 28 men brought in to meet him. I counted them. It was 'men only', we were told. The meeting took place in the monastery, outside his cell. We were told, 'We don't know what he will do. He may walk in, bless you and walk on, we don't know. He will definitely bless you but he may or may not also give the wounded hand to someone to kiss. We want to have everyone ready for this because it could be any of you.' They told us then, 'Stand up until he comes in, when he comes in kneel down, take your Rosaries and have them on your arm, medals in your hand and be perfectly still while he is with you.'

We waited for about ten minutes. Three or four Capuchin priests came in to where we were. We then heard the lift. Two monks, two Capuchin friars, linked him in. He was talking to them. At that stage he was close to 80 years old. He was dressed as a Capuchin friar. His hair was grey, as you'd see in the photos, magazines and books now. He couldn't speak English but he understood it and he said nothing to us.

He stayed with us for about eight to ten minutes. He just looked around and had a look at us all for a couple of seconds, then back again to talking away to his Capuchin friars for another few minutes. He turned around and gave another look. There was a great feeling of holiness there. He was a man that could read your mind and soul. Finally, they said, 'Hold up everything and he'll bless everything you have.' I held up Rosaries and medals. Like any priest, he blessed them.

Then he walked past each one of us. There was no ceremony. He just stood for a second before everyone and everybody touched his habit. I was the only one he handed the wounded hand to, to kiss. I couldn't have asked for more. I thought it was wonderful to be in the one room with him. It was the very same as if one was above in heaven. It was great to meet him in person and to kiss his hand. It was a great honour.

DONALD ENRIGHT ON HOW A CORK FAMILY RECEIVED GRACES AND BLESSINGS BY VISITING PADRE PIO.

Back in the 1960s a young child named Kieran, from Cork, was diagnosed with a medically incurable disease. His mother Margaret decided to bring him, along with her other son and her husband, to San Giovanni Rotondo. For financial reasons it was necessary for her to borrow £500. While at San Giovanni Rotondo her incurable child was blessed by Padre Pio and received his First Holy Communion from Padre Pio. They returned home with their child enjoying perfect health. They had only half a crown left out of the £500. Within a short time after arrival home she won £500, the exact amount of money she had borrowed.

A few years later Margaret was diagnosed as suffering from a malignant brain tumour. She was operated on in Dublin. The operation was only a partial success and within less than 12 months the tumour had regrown. She was left incurable and blind. Subsequent to medical advice she was hospitalised in St Patrick's Hospital, Wellington Road, Cork. While giving a talk on Padre Pio in Cork city I was asked to visit Margaret in the hospital and bless her with one of Padre Pio's mittens.

Almost immediately after I invoked Padre Pio's intercession on her behalf, she requested one of the nurses to provide her with St Patrick's Hospital headed paper. On that paper she wrote Padre Pio's name and full address in Italian without knowledge of the Italian language. Sight and health were restored to her from that moment. A while later, while giving a lecture in the Stardust Ballroom in Cork and showing slides of Padre Pio, I included a slide of the headed paper that Margaret wrote on. Within a few weeks I received a letter from her husband, who had been in the audience, in appreciation of reviving his wife and for bringing back happy memories of Padre Pio. I retain the letter and the headed paper to this day.

FATHER PIUS McLAUGHLIN OFM, WHO LIVES IN DUBLIN BUT WHO WAS REARED IN COUNTY DERRY, RELATES HOW HE CAME TO HAVE A LIFE-CHANGING CONFESSION WITH PADRE PIO IN 1967.

Having been professed as a Franciscan brother in 1962, I was sent from Ireland to the Irish Franciscan College, San Isidoro, in Rome. I worked there as a tailor for the next four years. Then, in 1966, out of the blue, I was assigned to an international Franciscan college in Florence. While I was there I was selected to attend the General Chapter of the Order in Assisi in May 1967. My basic task there was to assist the English-speaking provincials from all over the world, look after their needs and do translations for them.

One weekend a group of three of them wanted to go to San Giovanni Rotondo, to visit Padre Pio. They asked me to make arrangements and I travelled with them. We stayed in the friary there. We attended his Mass on the Saturday and the Sunday. On the Saturday afternoon they were anxious to get to Confession. He always heard Confessions for the men in the afternoon and the women in the morning. So I had the opportunity to go to Confession to him. I suppose that was the experience that transformed my life for ever.

I eventually found myself in the Confession box. I went in and I rattled off my Confession. As far as I remember, I hadn't very much to tell. Then there was a great silence. Nothing was happening and I was wondering was he there. He said to me, 'You didn't say you were a Franciscan lay brother.' I figured maybe he had seen the habit but there was nothing I had said that suggested that I was a religious and a Franciscan lay brother. That kind of shook me.

He followed it up by saying, 'Would you like to discuss your problem, and what are you going to do about it?' At that point I got very, very scared. I could feel myself breaking out into a sweat. I didn't know what to say. I said, 'I don't have a problem.' He said, 'You do.' I said, 'I don't.' He said, 'You do, and would you like to talk about it?' All this was in Italian. I had fluent Italian.

Then it dawned on me all of a sudden what he was talking about, which was that I had this notion that I would love to have been a priest. But I had no background educationally. I was a lay brother. It never had happened before that anyone went from that status to being a priest in the Irish province of the Order. He just said to me, 'I advise you to pray fervently, speak to your superior, humbly ask for permission, trust in God and leave the rest to him.'

That I did the following week when I went back to Assisi. I sat down with my provincial. He was shocked to hear me talk like this. He pointed out all these obstacles that were there. I outlined my desire. I said I understood about my background education, that it had never been done before. But I said, 'I'm willing to take this step and trust in God.' He said, 'OK, let's see what we can do.'

The rest is history. There were all kinds of obstacles that had to be overcome. I eventually went to America and I did all my studies. I did very, very well. I ended up with a Masters degree and was ordained a Franciscan priest in 1973.

I suppose if I were to take anything out of that personally, I would say that what I have learned and tried to live would be that there is a providence of God at work all the time. Nothing happens by chance. There are no coincidences. The other thing I learned was never to be afraid to risk; the fear of failure and the fear of risk keep all of us from jumping in. I have lived and worked out the notion of fear as being an acronym for 'false evidence appearing real'. I keep saying that to myself in every situation I find myself.

PATRICIA CONNOLLY, WHO LIVES IN YORKSHIRE BUT WHO ORIGINALLY CAME FROM COUNTY ROSCOMMON, TELLS THE STORY OF HER DECEASED HUSBAND JIM, FROM COUNTY FERMANAGH, WHO ONCE WENT TO CONFESSION WITH PADRE PIO AND WAS TOLD THAT HE WOULD DIE YOUNG.

In 1966 Jim went over to San Giovanni and met Padre Pio. He was 23 at the time. He was very religious and at one time was thinking about being a priest. In fact, he was maybe too religious to be a priest; he thought he wasn't good enough. Jim was devoted to Padre Pio. That's why he travelled. He had it in his mind to go.

He went to Confession with Padre Pio. Someone else, some Italian who was with him and who he had met up with, also went to Confession and Padre Pio told him that he hadn't told the whole truth. Padre Pio told Jim that he would die when he was very young. Padre Pio also put his hand on his head and a bit of blood went on his hair. He cut that piece of hair and carried it in his pocket until the day he died.

When I first met Jim he told me all about Padre Pio. He was really taken with him. He told me about the Confession. He used to joke about religion and say about himself, 'Look, I have lovely hands just like Padre Pio.' I don't know if he worried about Padre Pio although he might have worried inwardly. I never took any notice of the prediction because you never believe anyone is going to die at 33. You think they're going to live until 70 or 80 years.

We were married in 1972, in Italy, near San Giovanni in the parish of Jim's friend Don Carlo Carino. Our son Pio Emmanuel was born in 1974. Jim wanted him to be called Pio and we did call him that. When we went to sign the register he said, 'Pio.' Then the lady said to me, 'Do you want another name?' I said, 'Emmanuel' because I knew a nun in Strokestown who was very good to me when I was young and she was named Emmanuel. That evening Jimmy chucked me this book which was about Padre Pio. On the first page I opened, Padre Pio was referred to as Pio Emmanuel.

Then, at the age of 33, Jim had an accident in Newtownbutler. It was a car accident. We were living in England but he was always going over and back, mostly playing football. He was a very good footballer. They have a cup named after him. I was working in England and he had gone over from there. He was admitted to hospital. He was kept on a life-support machine in a Belfast hospital.

I went over and back. He was quite a few weeks unconscious and he eventually died at the age of 33, on the very same day that Padre Pio died and at the same time. It was 23 September, in the early hours of the morning. His mother was with him. It is quite a serious matter; you wonder about it, it is very strange.

I went to San Giovanni in 1997, when we would have been 25 years married. I went out with a group from Belfast. I was with Jim's cousin. It was very emotional. I just thought, 'Wouldn't it be nice if Jim was here.' I met Father Alessio, who had looked after Padre Pio, and he signed a prayer book for my son. I still keep in touch with his good friend Don Carlo Carino. The sad thing is that Jim was going to go back. If he had, he would have been there at Padre Pio's death in 1968.

I still live in England and my family have been here for years. I have never accepted Jim's death. I feel that he's in the house. Ever since he died I just keep moving house, it's just a reaction. I was very close to his mother and I visited her every year until she died. I am also close to Jim's family. My son Pio Emmanuel was brought up here but he loves Ireland and he lives there now.

I think it's very uncanny what happened to Jim and sometimes I am a bit frightened to pray to Padre Pio thinking things might go wrong. I pray to him but sometimes not too seriously just in case things may not turn out the right way. You wonder why Jim was killed, why he died on the date he did, how Emmanuel got his name. You wonder did Jim die for a good reason or a bad reason. I still think about it a lot.

STELLA ENRIGHT (NÉE MacSWEENEY), COUNTY KERRY, RECEIVED THE GIFT OF SIGHT AS A RESULT OF CORRESPONDENCE BETWEEN HER MOTHER AND PADRE PIO.
I was born a 24-week birth, a pound weight, at a time when there were no facilities like they have now. It was back in 1956. The doctor, at the time, said I wouldn't survive. But my parents wrapped me in a blanket, got me into the car and they drove me to hospital in Galway. I was turning blue as I arrived. They had an incubator ready and they put me into it. Obviously, I survived.

I wasn't allowed home for quite a while after that. Then, when I got to about six or seven months, they noticed that I wasn't taking account of what was going on around me. My mother went back to the doctor but he kind of fobbed her off. They then did tests on the back of my eyes and they said, 'The most she will ever see will be a chair, it will have to be the biggest chair and it will just be a shadow.' They said the optical nerves were blown in my two eyes and they couldn't be repaired.

My parents were devastated. They took me to see Father Peyton when he came to Knock. Then, when I came to about a year or two years, my mother read this article about Padre Pio who was a priest in San Giovanni. He wasn't widely known at the time. My father had an aunt who was a nun in Tralee. My mother asked her if she would be able to make contact with Padre Pio. Through a nun, through another nun, through the convent they made contact. Within a short time a little medal came from San Giovanni, which I have to this day.

The medal was sewn into a scapular. Every day my mother used to put me up on her lap. She would put the medal up to the left eye, there would be no reaction. She would put it up to the right eye, again no reaction. She did this for a few weeks. One day she put it up to the left eye and there was no reaction. But when she put it up to the right eye, for the first time I put my hand up and tried to grab it. My mother couldn't believe it. She said nothing. She did it a few more times and the same thing happened. From that day on, I began to see.

As I grew up, my sight grew with me. I could see as much as I needed to see. They wanted to put me into a school for the blind. But my mother said, 'She is going to lead a normal life, like a normal girl.' So they put me into ordinary school. I used to get up from my chair, walk up to the blackboard to read what was on it, memorise three words at a time, come down and write them down. That's how I did my study, and I did well.

When I was about eight or nine years of age, I remember I was due to go to Dublin for an eye test. The day before we were to travel, this parcel came in the door which we hadn't sent for. It wasn't asked for. We didn't even know where Padre Pio lived; only that he lived in Italy. We didn't know whether to open it or not because we didn't even believe it was for us. We opened it and there was a little Rosary beads inside, in a little case, and a little card. I don't know whether he wrote it himself or not but it said on the back, 'For dear little Stella, say the Rosary every day.' Padre Pio obviously knew what was going on. I have it since.

As I got older I did a secretarial course. I got a job in an office. I did a full day's work, running an office, doing the typing and the reception. That was all on the vision I had. I could do it all on so little. My eyes were fine. Ever since then I have had devotion to Padre Pio. He is still there with me and I am depending on him for what I have.

KATHLEEN O'SULLIVAN, COUNTY KERRY, WROTE LETTERS TO PADRE PIO ASKING FOR FAVOURS AND ADVICE.

I read a book about Padre Pio around 1945 or 1946. I wasn't married then. I was a young girl, about 19. I don't know what came over me. I can't explain what it did to me. I couldn't wait to get to the end of the book. I used to stay up all night long, sitting in the chair, reading it. He took me over completely.

I grew to absolutely love the man. I don't know what attracted me to him. I got this feeling that if I ever was in real dire trouble that Padre Pio would take me up to the top of the cliff and, just when he was ready to throw me in, he would pull back. He would try you out.

I then started writing to him. I was always looking for something in life. I was looking for things like guidance in my married life and for material things. I wrote umpteen times to him, countless times. One letter I got from him he answered himself. He told me to pray, hope and don't worry and that everything was in the hands of God through the intercession of Our Blessed Lady. After that, the replies were sent by one of the friars.

My eldest daughter got rheumatic fever when she was about 12 or 13. One night she was up in her room studying. She said to me, 'I don't want supper tonight.' I said, 'Come on, come on, the food is on the table.' She admitted to me then that she couldn't walk. I said, 'What's wrong with you?' 'I don't know,' she said, 'but I have pains all over me and I only have a little power in my hands.'

The doctor came out. He said to me that she had rheumatic fever. She also had a murmur in her heart. The doctor said to forget about her studies, she was so sick. I didn't realise how sick she was. I was very worried. We nursed her ourselves at home. I was praying to Padre Pio. I also sent off my few shillings to him, which was difficult at the time with all the forms you had to fill in at the bank.

After about a month the doctor came out and checked her and he could not find a thing. He said the murmur was cleared. He checked her for her temperature as well, which was fine. That very day I got a letter, an answer, back from Padre Pio saying that he was praying for me and for my daughter. Inside of the letter was a lovely picture of Our Lady of Grace. I brought it up to my daughter that evening and she cried with joy. I said, 'You are going to be better, that's a letter from Padre Pio.' It was what always happened; you'd always get your request before the letters would come. I have that letter all the time since.

KAY THORNTON ALSO WROTE TO PADRE PIO.

I probably wrote dozens of times to him asking for favours. I wrote and I asked him would he accept me as one of his spiritual children. I wanted him to be looking after me. I waited for months and months. I was in a terrible state. I thought he was going to refuse me. The next thing, I got a letter with big blue print on it saying that Padre Pio accepted me as a spiritual child and asking me to pray for him. I still have all the letters including the one accepting me as his spiritual child.

THE AUNT OF DUBLIN RESIDENT ROSALYN O'MAHONEY RECEIVED A LETTER FROM THE FRIARY AT SAN GIOVANNI BACK IN 1964.

My aunt, Sister Barbara McCarthy, was a nun. Back in the 1960s she got cancer of the throat and she prayed and prayed especially to Padre Pio. There was no hope originally. One day she was taken in for this very serious operation. She said to the surgeon, 'I'm praying for you.' He said, 'If you say that one more time to me! Don't pray for me. Any time you say that to me I have no luck afterwards.'

My Uncle Brendan said to me that this surgeon was a complete atheist. When he did the operation a second time, it was a success and she was fine. Afterwards, she said to him, 'Oh, thank you so much, thank you, thank you.' She was afraid to say, 'I'm praying for you.' She said, 'You really are a miracle.' 'Oh, no,' he said, 'it's not me this time; it's that other fellow you have.'

She used to write to us all the time and she had a great interest in all of us. She was a beautiful writer, with beautiful handwriting and beautiful English. Then, some years ago, Sister Barbara died having lived a further 35 years or so. About two years later my father was very ill and he was going for an operation. He gave me everything he had. He handed me this letter and said, 'This is very precious to me.' It was just a little page, authentic and bound in Sellotape because it was so old. He said, 'You mind that, you keep that.'

It was from the Convento dei Cappuccini, San Giovanni Rotondo. It's dated August 1964, it's to Sister Barbara and it says, 'Padre Pio sends you his blessing and will pray for your intentions. He urges you to have complete trust in the goodness of God and to pray always according to His Divine Will. Padre also thanks you for your offering.' It's signed 'Father Superior'.

It's a nice thing to have. Sister Barbara believed in him for a long time after that and she lived on well into her 80s. She had a beautiful death although she did eventually die of throat cancer. The letter is a treasured possession. It's lovely to have.

MARY BRIODY, NIECE OF MAIREAD DOYLE, OUTLINES HOW PADRE PIO INTERVENED WHEN HER NEWBORN SISTER WAS FACED WITH DEATH IN THE MID-1960s.

When my sister Deirdre, who was the youngest in the family, was born she had three cerebral haemorrhages. The doctors didn't give her any hope. Daddy was told to order the white coffin. He came home and told us that the baby wasn't going to live. We said the Rosary at home. Mairead had this relic of Padre Pio at the time and she put the relic on my sister and sent a telegram to San Giovanni.

Of course, Deirdre did get better. So Mairead wrote to, or sent a telegram to, Padre Pio and said she would bring my sister over when she was four. Padre Pio's reply was, 'I've already been with Deirdre.' She didn't bring her at four because Mammy wouldn't allow her, but she did bring her at eight.

DONALD ENRIGHT ATTENDED NUMEROUS MASSES OF PADRE PIO IN SAN GIOVANNI.

Padre Pio arose at two o'clock in the morning. That's if he went to bed at all. He prayed until half past four in preparation for his Mass. From the moment he entered the sacristy, the white mittens he wore by night were removed and his wrists were swathed in bandages to prevent the blood from his stigmatised hands from falling onto his vestments.

He staggered forward on his stigmatised feet onto the altar where Our Blessed Lady accompanied him every morning for his Mass. He once said, 'Poor little Mother, how much she loves me, she makes me feel as if I were her only child on earth.' He also said, 'Poor little Mother, how lovingly she accompanies me onto the altar this morning, it seems that she has nobody else to think of except myself alone.'

The church was packed every morning with approximately 2,000 people. You realised that there were also 2,000 guardian angels in that church. One morning, during the month of October 1960, I arrived outside the entrance to the church to take my place in the queue, awaiting the opening of the doors. I counted 50 separate buses bringing people to the Mass. That didn't include people travelling by car or local people walking from the town of San Giovanni.

From the moment his Mass commenced, you saw the love on his face but it quickly changed to a face of agony. Shortly after the Mass started the blood poured from his hands. He would have no mittens on. The wounds would burst open and the blood would pour out. On occasions, the blood from his stigmatised hand mingled with the blood of Jesus Christ in the chalice.

He prayed, begged and pleaded during his Mass to relieve Jesus of his sufferings and to take on those sufferings. He prayed for the sick and suffering. He saw in the sick and suffering the mystical body of Christ twice over. Nothing was good enough for the sick. He also prayed for those in need, especially for the salvation of souls. As he gazed on the host in his hand, his look changed from one of terrible agony to one of adoration and love. You could feel the palpitations of his heart through his intense love for the body and blood of Jesus he was about to receive.

Sometimes, when sins of the world were revealed to him during his Mass, he would cry and he would have to make use of what was known as a 'tear cloth' or a towel to wipe his eyes. He was begging and pleading all the time to relieve Jesus of his suffering. Occasionally he spoke in a language which I didn't understand; it was the language Jesus spoke when he walked the Holy Land. Padre Pio also died mystically during his Mass and it was the arms of St Francis that supported his body. At that time his arms were outstretched in an upward movement identical to a crucified person.

He said of the host, 'When I receive the host I do not know if the heart of Jesus is infused into my heart or if it is my heart that is infused into the heart of Jesus.' Such was the intensity of his love. Due to the stigmata on his feet he was not allowed to distribute Communion to the public. But children receiving First Holy Communion received it from the hands of Padre Pio because of his love for the innocence and beauty of those about to receive the body of Christ for the first time.

The Mass lasted until half past six and you couldn't hear

one cough in the church due to the love of the people for Padre Pio as they joined him in prayer. Sometimes he would speak to one or more people during his Mass, as he did one morning. He spoke to a man who came in on crutches as a result of an accident. One leg could not bend. He turned to the man and said, 'Stand up and throw away your crutches.' The man did not, so Padre Pio repeated, 'Oh, you of little faith, stand up and throw away your crutches.' The man stood and he found he could bend his knee as he could in years gone by. The man literally danced for joy in the church that morning.

He prayed on his knees for 20 minutes after his Mass. Men were allowed into the sacristy to join him. There might be 200 or 300 in the sacristy. Everybody would be on their knees. He would bless them sometimes in a general way. At other times he would pick out one or two people. He would touch a few of the people with his hands. He would give you the back of his hand to kiss, with the mitten on.

His Masses were very moving. I cried and shed tears looking at him suffering. I cried profusely morning after morning. I felt totally and utterly unworthy to be in his presence. I also felt it was my sins, and the sins of people like me, that caused Padre Pio to suffer. It also made me realise that Jesus died on the cross for my sins and for the salvation of our souls. His Masses were never to be forgotten.

MONA HANAFIN ADDS HER ACCOUNT OF PADRE PIO'S MASS. I expected that he would be like a film star, such a wonderful man coming out on the altar. But when I saw him coming out, trying to walk and with the priests holding onto him, I just knew he was a saint. His shoe size was a size eight but his feet were so swollen with the blood that they looked like a size twelve. He had a wonderful presence about him. It wasn't a 'show' presence; it was a 'humility' presence of pain and prayer and gentleness. You knew as soon as you saw him that he was a saint.

At the Consecration you felt that he was talking to Jesus. They say that he was talking to Jesus and that the Lord would give him souls to take care of. One day he said how wonderful it was that Our Lady had accompanied him on the altar. Seemingly, she did that nearly every day. You'd know by his eyes that he was looking not at the host but at something way beyond that. His eyes were aglow and glazed over as he was concentrating on the host. You knew it wasn't the host but that there was somebody there.

FATHER PIUS McLAUGHLIN OFM ALSO DESCRIBES PADRE PIO'S MASS.

This man came out of the sacristy walking slowly to this rustic altar. The mittens were off. He began the Mass. It was like he was on the cross with Christ. The suffering in all of his body, but particularly in his hands and his feet, was obvious to everyone that was in that church. The expression on his face told it all, there was this kind of a glowing fire and then his pallid complexion turned into what was almost fear.

Other times he was tearful. And his voice! It was as if he was presiding in some other-worldly atmosphere different to ours, on another level of humanity different to where we were. I truly believe that the altar was his own personal Calvary where he lived out the mystery of the death and resurrection of Christ. You knew he was speaking with God right through that Mass, at every moment of it. You were witnessing an intense love and, at the same time, tremendous suffering.

The other thing was that you became conscious of a feeling of warmth around you. It was as though love was filling every space, even the very breath that you were inhaling. All around you was still. I have never been in a situation like that before or since. There wasn't even the sound of breathing. Everything was held in a kind of suspension. You glanced at others and you could see tears trickling unashamedly down people's faces, and down my own. Then one became aware of one's own failings.

I just can't describe the Consecration; the pain was so great at that moment. It was very difficult for him to even repeat the words of Consecration. Remember, he was saying the Mass in Latin. At the elevation of the chalice and the host he definitely was in another world. Having been at Confession with him, I felt that he was bringing my needs and what weakness I had, and my desire to be what I wanted to be, right to the Lord and saying, 'You look after him.' I can then remember the peace and calm that settled over his pain-wracked face immediately after he received Communion.

It was certainly the most unforgettable experience of my life. It was an experience that would stir the very depths of your soul. This experience of what was going on in front of me set me aflame. Yet not one word was preached. It was the experience of being there for over two hours, on both occasions, but one didn't even know that the time had passed. To me his Mass was a visible and tangible sign of what his mission and his spirituality and his life were all about. Everybody knew that something different was happening. You couldn't attend it without going away saying, 'That was an experience I've had that I'll never have again.'

MIRACULOUS EVENTS

ARGUABLY NO OTHER SAINT INTERCEDES AS tellingly as Padre Pio. Certainly in modern times, no other wonder-worker is as widely revered for securing graces and blessings from God. In Ireland alone, thousands of miraculous cures and life-changing incidents have been attributed to the friar's intercessions. Many of these supernatural occurrences have followed from prayers appealing for his help. Others have transpired after the touching of a relic, often one of his mittens. Some of the graces have been instantaneously received; more have been bestowed over time.

Sometimes the achievement is the attainment of conversion, peace or tranquillity. More frequently, people claim relief, or cures, from a vast range of serious and at times potentially fatal illnesses. This chapter features recoveries from brain tumours, lung cancer, colon cancer and Hodgkin's disease. Revivals are documented by people who once suffered from multiple sclerosis and bone disease. Paralysis, strokes, haemorrhages, mysterious viruses, arthritis and heart defects have all been overcome. Even depression has been successfully defeated.

As with all of the cures historically attributed to Padre Pio, these reputed miracles accord with particular patterns. Some involve full recoveries with the disappearance of the original signs and symptoms. In other cases, clinical evidence remains unchanged but the resulting diminution of pain and suffering can legitimately be referred to as a cure. Not infrequently, medical opinion is baffled by the unfolding course of events. Experts are regularly unable to offer suggestions as to what might have happened, referring instead to developments as being medically inexplicable.

MAUREEN BRODERICK, LIMERICK, ON THE SURVIVAL OF ONE OF HER TWINS, JACK.

In March 2001 I gave birth to twins, Jack and Beth. Everything was fine. There were no complications. When they came home from hospital they had a touch of gastroenteritis. Beth rallied around and it never really bothered her much. But every now and then it would flare up with Jack. Coming up to Christmas, Jack seemed to get a particularly bad dose of it. He was keeping absolutely nothing down, no food, no bottles, no water, nothing. We had him with the doctor and the hospital and they all said, 'No, no, take him home, he's grand.'

On Christmas Eve night everybody had gone to bed bar me. I was doing Santa. I put Jack up to bed about the two o'clock mark. He got sick. I thought, 'Oh, God, I'm wrecked and I'm never going to get up in the morning.' I cleaned him up and my husband said, 'Look, you go out of the room and when he can't see you he'll go back to sleep.' Five minutes later I thought, 'He's too quiet, I'm going to check him.' He appeared to be having a fit of some description.

We got him to the hospital. My sister-in-law is a nurse, she lived across the road and she said, 'Jump in the car, it's quicker than getting an ambulance.' So we went to the hospital and after a period of about four hours they were able to stop the fit. His body was convulsing the whole time; he was having mini-strokes. They weren't able to give us a lot of information about what was wrong with him but they thought he might have meningitis.

By the end of that Christmas Day we knew there had been some trauma in his head but we didn't know how serious it was. On St Stephen's Day we had him moved to Cork and within 24 hours of being in Cork they told us he had two massive bleeds in his head. As the brain tried to stop the bleeding, a massive clot had formed in the top of his head. It was quite apparent, as his forehead was bulging. They didn't know what they could do for us. All this time, Jack was in a coma.

Eventually, the doctors told us they were very sorry but that there was nothing they could do and that if we wanted to lift him out of the cot we could. They also told us that if there was other family, his twin sister, his older sister, to come down, it was the time to do it. My husband and I were very shocked. Never for a moment had it dawned on us that this was what we were facing. We thought they were going to be able to help us and sort it out.

My sister rang and said, 'I've heard of this guy who has a relic of Padre Pio. Will I get him to call to you?' At the time, I wouldn't have known much about Padre Pio. He hadn't yet been canonised. I said, 'Do, I will do anything to get my son to where I want him to be.' About an hour later there was a knock on the door and this gentleman came in with the relic. From the minute he came into the room there was a sense of relief, we were very calm and we were told that we had to look at it from God's point of view.

Jack was blessed with the relic and the relic was placed under his pillow where the initial brain haemorrhage was, down along the left side. The gentleman spoke to us for about forty minutes and he left us coming up to about ten o'clock. An hour after the gentleman left, Jack woke up. He called for my mother, 'Nana.' When he did, my husband Damien jumped up off the floor. Jack looked at my husband and he said, 'Dad, Dad,' and he fell back to sleep.

We called the doctors and the nurses and we were basically told that often, just before death, the person about to die will come around. They said this was a last rally and to expect to lose him during the night. Jack remained unconscious after that for another 48 hours and when he woke up he threw a teddy out the side of the cot. I ran out and called the nurses and doctors. The next thing, there was bedlam because they couldn't believe this child was alive and awake. They said, 'He may not be able to pull through, this may be just a final stage.' They tried to tell us to not get our hopes up too high. Ten days later we were bringing him back to Limerick.

We were up and down to Dublin after that and eventually, six months later, one of the doctors told us, 'Take your son home. I don't know how he's alive. I have never known anyone with this much brain damage to live. He shouldn't be here.' Today I have a five-year-old son who is top of his class in school, who is very popular and has a great charisma around him. Nobody can tell us exactly what happened to him and none of the medics can explain how he is alive. My only explanation is that Padre Pio entered our lives and he definitely brought Jack back to us.

JOSEPHINE Mc LAUGHLIN, COUNTY DONEGAL, RECALLS HER SON BILL'S RECOVERY FROM A NEAR-FATAL CAR ACCIDENT.
Bill went to work as usual one All Souls' Day back in the mid-1990s. He was 23 at the time. He was coming home that evening. I was waiting for him with his dinner but he never turned up. We finished our dinner. Then the Guards knocked at the door of the house and came on in. They were friends of ours and friends of Bill's. They told us that he had an accident; that we'd need to go to the hospital right away but not to worry. They didn't want to tell us the extent of it.

The Guards pieced together what had happened. Bill was

driving from work on a narrow back road. The wheels of
the car caught the grass on the verge and he lost control. He
hit a bridge and went out through the roof and fell back in
again. There was a sun-roof in the car. He was then lying in
the passenger seat. It was a back road with no traffic on it.
This lady came along who was visiting her father's grave on
All Souls' Day. She had a wee boy in the back seat. She passed
the car and thought the crash had happened a long time ago.
But the wee boy looked behind, as they passed, and he said,
'Mommy, there's a light or something in that car.' So she came
back to investigate.

She found Bill and went to get help. In the meantime,
another lady came along who was a nurse in intensive care. She
stopped and had a look. She found that he was actually dead,
his heart had stopped. She worked on him and resuscitated
him. It so happened that there was an ambulance only about
five minutes away and they came to the scene of the crash.
The doctor came also. The ambulance-men were trying to put
a collar on his neck but the doctor told them to leave him
alone, trying to keep him alive was more important at that
time.

The ambulance then took him to Letterkenny where they
had great difficulty keeping him stable. He passed away
a couple of times. Nothing was stable, including his blood
pressure. They sent him then by helicopter, in the morning,
to Beaumont in Dublin. We arrived up that afternoon and the
doctor was waiting for us. He told us that there was only a
50 per cent chance that he would survive and that, if he did
survive, he would be a vegetable. They had him sedated and
they had him in theatre. It was dreadful.

Somebody told me about the Padre Pio mitt. I went and I
got it from Eileen Maguire at the Padre Pio office. I brought
the mitt back and rubbed it on Bill and said prayers. I was
given a wee leaflet and I kept saying those prayers all the time.

I was grasping at straws, to be quite honest with you. I had no belief in Padre Pio at that stage. The next day he came out of the coma. It was great although he was paralysed on the left side from the top of the head to the top of the big toe. He couldn't move at all. Even his eye was closed. He didn't know anybody and he had no coordination. If you gave him a bowl of jelly he was as liable to put it in his ears as his mouth.

Somebody then told me that there was a wee monk in the hospital. It turned out his name was Brother Laurence, a Capuchin from Raheny. He had Padre Pio's mitt with him. I thought to myself, 'I will get it again because Bill came out of the coma with it the first time.' This was all running through my mind. I went looking for Brother Laurence. He was only a wee man; you could have put him in your pocket he was that small. He was lovely. I asked him to come and see Bill and he said he would. So he came and he rubbed the mitt all over him. He then gave it to us to bless ourselves with. He said, 'It will be alright, he is too young to be left like that.'

About 15 minutes after he left the ward, the first thing Bill did was lift his leg right up the whole way. He lifted his arm and put his hand across his chest. I called the nurse and she came in. She called the doctor and he said to me that he didn't understand it. He said that, normally, with someone paralysed like that it would be just a wee twitch to start with and then you'd have to work on it.

Despite the progress, a day or two later Bill still didn't know us. I was sitting by his bed and the nurse said, 'There's a telephone call for you.' I got up to take the call and when I was halfway across the floor I heard, 'Mammy, where are you going?' It was a husky voice. Needless to say I never answered the phone. I came back, I couldn't believe it. Bill got everything back every day after that.

He came back to 100 per cent normal. They had him booked for rehabilitation in Dun Laoghaire. He never had to go. They also had him booked into Letterkenny for physiotherapy. When I took him in the physiotherapist called his name. He and I walked in. She looked around and said, 'It's not you I am looking for, it's Bill Mc Laughlin.' I said, 'This is Bill Mc Laughlin.' She looked at her notes again and said, 'According to these notes it's not, he should be in a wheelchair.' He went down to our own doctor in Buncrana. He calls a spade a spade. When Bill walked in he was reading the notes that had come down from Dublin. He looked at Bill and said, 'You should be dead.' Bill said, 'Well, I am here.' Even when the doctors did tests they said, 'You shouldn't be able to do what you are able to do.'

Later, we got a notice to go up to Beaumont for a check-up. Bill and I travelled up and he drove. We went in. They gave him a brain scan before he went in to see the neurologist. When we went in the neurologist was reading the scan. He started to talk to me, 'How is he?' I said, 'He's fine, he's grand.' 'Tell me,' he said, 'can he put on his own clothes?' I was taken aback and said, 'He can.' 'He doesn't put them on outside in or anything like that?' he asked. I said, 'No, as a matter of fact he drove all the way from Donegal this morning.' He looked at Bill in surprise and started to talk to him then. At the end I asked him, 'Why is he the way he is, so perfect, after such an accident?' 'I can't explain it,' he said, 'it's not anything we did; it has to be divine intervention.'

During that first check-up we drove out to Raheny to visit Brother Laurence. We had a great evening with him. He was amusing. He would rub Bill's chin and say, 'Lovely chin for a beard!' We went up a few times to see him but then he got a stroke about a year to the day after Bill had the accident. He eventually passed away. The mitt has never been found.

If Bill has a brain scan it still shows up all the injuries and the part of the brain that is gone. But there are no symptoms. They even had him booked for a small operation for his throat because the tubes had damaged his vocal cords. That was why he sounded so hoarse the first time he spoke to me. He didn't even have to have that. The only thing he might have is a difficulty with people's names.

It had to be Padre Pio. The story was recorded in San Giovanni. Bill also went to Padre Pio's beatification, which was very important to him. Bill and I and a friend, Father Joe, then went out to San Giovanni in thanksgiving after Padre Pio's canonisation. Father Joe celebrated Mass on his tomb, on Bill's birthday. The monks presented Bill with a relic, a small piece of bandage. If anybody wants it he will bring it to them, it doesn't matter where to. But he won't part with it or give it to anybody. We are both devotees now. We are not fanatics. But we are ever so thankful to Padre Pio for what he did.

SEAN MULRINE, DERRY, DESCRIBES HOW PADRE PIO SAVED HIS WIFE'S LIFE. SEAN RUNS THE PADRE PIO CENTRE FOR NORTHERN IRELAND, WHICH IS AFFILIATED TO THE MONASTERY AT SAN GIOVANNI ROTONDO.

One Sunday morning, 26 years ago, my wife and I were planning to go on a picnic to a local beauty spot. After we finished our dinner Ann went into the sitting-room with a cup of coffee. The two older children, Michael and Nichola, and I started to prepare a picnic hamper. At this point Ann was pregnant with twins. While we were making the picnic hamper we heard a scream from the sitting-room. I ran in to find Ann lying on the floor.

A few years before that, Ann had miscarried a child. I thought it was something to do with this happening again. We called a doctor. By the time the doctor came Ann was completely stiff, her eyes were rolling in her head and her mouth was twisted up to her ear. The doctor got a pair of scissors to cut the clothes off Ann and gave her several injections. The ambulance came and took her to the local hospital.

A team of doctors and nurses examined her while I sat in the waiting-room. They came to me and said, 'Mr Mulrine, your wife has no more than half an hour to live. She either had a massive brain haemorrhage or has a tumour of the brain. We just don't know but we feel that's most probably what it is.' They said, 'If you wish, we can keep your wife alive by ventilator until the unborn children reach the age of 38 weeks, which is about two and a half months away. If you don't sign the forms, then your wife and two unborn children will die within the next half-hour.'

I signed the forms and they told me to go in and say goodbye, she might or might not hear me. I went in but she was just like an animal, there was blood coming from everywhere, she was completely distorted. Then they took her away and put her on the life-support machine. She looked as if she was lying peacefully after that.

That night I went down to visit my mother and my mother-in-law and I was handed a little relic leaflet of Padre Pio by my mother. That was the first time I ever heard of him. I shoved it in my top pocket. I then went back up to our house to make arrangements for the children to be looked after. I went, after that, to arrange for time off work. The man we had bought our house off had roses everywhere in the front garden and when I was passing them I thought, 'I will take those roses to Our Lady's altar.' But I sort of laughed at it and walked away.

Eventually I was walking through a place called William Street where there's a beautiful flower shop. The window was full of roses. Once again I got this feeling that I should take flowers to Our Lady's altar. So I went in and bought some and took them up to the chapel. As I was putting the roses on the altar the stems of the flowers caught the little leaflet I had been given. It was sticking out of my pocket and it fell to the ground. I lifted it up and knelt down and said the prayer on it, which was a prayer Padre Pio would have said for people looking for his intercession. It said everything you would have liked to have said but didn't know how to say. From that time on I had a great prayerfulness about me, which I never had before.

Ten or twelve days passed and Ann was still the same. One night I was sitting down beside her with the little leaflet and I said, 'Look, if you're going to do something for me, give me a sign.' I asked Ann to squeeze my hand and I swore she did. I sent for the nurse and the doctor but they told me I was clutching at straws, there was no chance at all. They said she was clinically brain dead. But they said there was a specialist coming down in a few days and he would talk to me and put me more clearly in the picture.

Eventually this doctor came down and told me what I had been told before. He said, 'Your wife either had a massive brain haemorrhage or has a tumour and we have no intention of doing anything at all because your wife is clinically dead, only the machine is keeping the children going.' Another five or six weeks passed. All this time I was going to Our Lady's altar with roses and praying to Padre Pio. They then asked me could they move my wife to hospital in Belfast and I said, 'Yes.'

One night in Belfast I was sitting beside my wife's bed when one of the nurses said, 'Mr Mulrine, would you mind leaving for a while?' It was about half past one or two o'clock in the morning. I went down to the end of the corridor and I started saying the Rosary. I got up after the first decade and walked towards Ann's bed but something pulled me back. On the last decade of the Rosary I looked up the corridor and I saw this figure coming around the corner and I ran towards it and said, 'Excuse me, you're looking for me.'

I had never met the man in my life, I didn't know who the man was; don't ask me why I said that. He said, 'I'm looking for a man called Mulrine.' I said, 'That's me.' The man's name was Michael Murray and he and his wife ran the Padre Pio Centre for Northern Ireland. He said, 'I got a phone call about half an hour ago from a lady who said for me to take the glove of Padre Pio to Sean and Ann Mulrine in the Royal Hospital.' This was a brown mitt that Padre Pio would have had over the bandages, over the stigmata on his hands. We went up to Ann and he said to me, 'She might hear you talking, tell her what it is.' So I told her.

We put the glove of Padre Pio on Ann's head. Despite all the tubes, she moved her hand, she grabbed the glove, she brought the glove to her face, blessed herself three times, brought it to her stomach and blessed her stomach with it. She then just fell back into the bed again. This was the first movement we had seen. After that, Michael and I sat and he told me some things about Padre Pio. Then we left. I went to my room. Next morning I went to Ann's bed again but she was moved and the bed was gone. I thought they had taken her to take the children out. The nurse came to me and said, 'The doctors have read the reports from last night and they've taken her down to surgery for exploratory examination.'

They removed part of the crown of her head and put a camera in to see what was there. They came to me after the operation and said they had seen several of the major vessels in the brain and they had burst. There was a large amount of congealed blood in the centre of the brain and it could not be sucked out. They said, 'We don't know how the event last night happened, we can't understand it, she's clinically dead.' That night I went into my room and I couldn't go through the door for the overpowering smell of roses. It was years later that I was told that this was the invisible presence of Padre Pio.

To cut a long story short, Ann came out of the recovery room, they put her in bed and she opened her eyes and started to talk and move. They took her off the ventilator to see how she would do. They called it a fluke. They said, 'We don't know how this has happened.' Ann got so well that she was eventually brought back to Derry, where the babies were born just a week after she arrived. She just went from strength to strength. She never looked back and she and the two boys were released from hospital on 23 September, which was the anniversary of the death of Padre Pio.

Eventually we went out to San Giovanni in thanksgiving and we met Father Alessio who was Padre Pio's secretary and nurse. He is dead since. He asked could he investigate Ann's story as part of the cause of Padre Pio. They investigated for four or five years or more. When they asked for the doctors' personal opinions, they all said it was beyond medical science how she is today.

As a result, for the beatification we were asked to meet the Pope and present flowers from the people of Ireland. And for the canonisation I was also invited to go up to the Pope with the presentations. We take the trips out now in thanksgiving. We never make any fuss about it. We don't say it was a miracle. We say it was a grace given by God through the intercession of Padre Pio.

GEMMA DILLON, COUNTY MEATH, REGAINED THE USE OF HER LEG FOLLOWING A VISIT TO SAN GIOVANNI.
In 1976 I had unsuccessful hip surgery and, as a result, one leg didn't work. They had severed a main nerve during surgery and I was on crutches. My leg was hanging loose. I was dragging it behind me. Two years later, in 1978, we moved back from England, bought a small business and we had a week before we took it over. So we went on holiday to Rome. It was at the time of the death of Pope John Paul I and the election was taking place of Pope John Paul II. It was packed and crowded in Rome, really crammed. We were there for the white smoke and all that.

We had gone to Rome on a trip which was going to both Rome and San Giovanni. When we got to Rome we were given the option of staying there. I had loosely heard of Padre Pio but I had no interest. We decided to stay in Rome. However, the morning the group were leaving we were going out of our hotel and I tumbled down the steps because of the crowds and because I wasn't nimble on my feet. Eddie, my husband, hauled me up and said, 'I think we had better get out of Rome or you will be killed.' So we said to the organisers, 'I think we will go down to this other place, wherever it is.'

In San Giovanni we did all the things that pilgrims do. The people on the trip said, 'We'll have to get you blessed.' I was saying, 'Yeah.' One of the days, there was a very old priest, Father Romolo, and he blessed everybody who was in the choir loft at twelve o'clock. I was hauled up there. We waited around and some people pushed me across and he blessed me. I was barely interested and I just carried on. Later, I went into Father Alessio's office and he took the mitten and gave me a blessing. At this stage I was kind of interested in spite of myself.

Later that day I said to myself in a jesting way, 'I could have a miracle here, for all I know.' Up to then I had been dragging the leg along and I had two crutches. Strangely, as I was walking I was saying, 'That leg feels not too bad.' By the time I got back down to our hotel I was trying it out gently on my own, thinking it was a lot of nonsense and imagination on my part. When I got up to the room I said, 'I think the leg is better.' I was standing on it and moving it. I put the crutches down and I was walking up and down the room. We were wildly excited.

When we went to dinner I took the crutches. I didn't want to say anything yet. That night I was afraid to go to sleep in case I woke up the next morning and the strength in my leg would be gone. But it wasn't, the next morning the strength was still there. I showed people how I could walk with one crutch. By the time I left San Giovanni, less than a week later, I was walking without any crutches.

I believe it was Padre Pio. At the time it happened I had lost complete faith. I had gone in for a simple procedure to my hip and it went wrong, leaving my leg literally dead. In spite of everybody's prayers and novenas, nothing seemed to be happening. It wasn't until I went to San Giovanni that something happened. Even that was by accident, after my fall in Rome.

A few months later I went back in thanksgiving to San Giovanni with another group. I had no crutches, just a walking-stick in case I got tired. I said to Father Alessio, 'Look at me, do you not remember that I came in here and I couldn't walk?' He said, 'This happens all the time. Now you must take a film of Padre Pio and travel around Ireland and tell people.' I had never shown a film in all my life or spoken in public. So I took the film, came back home, and over the following ten years I don't think there was a part of Ireland that I didn't visit.

MARIE DURACK, COUNTY CLARE, ON PADRE PIO'S ROLE IN MAKING HER WELL AND BRINGING HER A BABY GIRL.

Thirty years ago I had my second baby, a boy. Before he was born I got a very bad sore throat. After the baby was born I got very sick and I didn't know what was after happening to me. I spent two months in the hospital with my kidneys damaged and a clot on my lung. I was on twenty-four tablets and six or eight injections a day. They told me I was going to be a long time in hospital. I had to have complete bed rest.

I got Tom Cooney, a Padre Pio devotee, to come in to me with Padre Pio's glove. When he came in he rubbed the glove on me. I also prayed to Padre Pio. I was there eight weeks. It was so bad at one stage that there were about 23 doctors around my bed trying to figure out what was wrong with me.

Then, suddenly, during Holy Week the doctor came in and said, 'There's something after happening here, get her out of bed and get her walking.' That was Holy Week and by Good Friday I was home out of hospital.

They gave me the strongest tablets they could give me and said, 'If these tablets don't work within eight weeks, you are on the kidney machine.' I went up and down to Tom Cooney. One night he said to me, 'With the help of God you'll be OK.' The following Friday morning I went back in to the doctor for my eight-week check-up and he said, 'There's been a great improvement, everything has disappeared.' I never got a kidney infection after that.

They also told me that there was never again to be any more children. I got a letter saying to go down to Cork to tie my tubes. They told me that if I went back and had another baby the same thing would happen all over again. So I went down to Tom Cooney again and told him my story. I said to him, 'I don't think I can go ahead with this.' Always at the back of my mind I thought sometime I might have a baby girl. So I didn't have my tubes tied. They also kept me coming back for four years. I kept praying away to Padre Pio, thanking him for giving back my health. At the end of that time they told me, 'Everything is perfect.'

A nurse that nursed me asked would I go out to Padre Pio's tomb. I went out with her in thanksgiving for everything being so good. I prayed at his tomb and stood at every statue out there and I said, 'Thanks, Padre Pio, for everything but I'd love a baby girl.' That was October and the following July, nine months later, Regina was born. I called her Regina Mary Pia. So I had my daughter and I had a second one, Gillian Marie Pia, five years later. That's after being told never to have any more.

Nothing ever happened to me ever again and I really and truly believe that Padre Pio was responsible. I also believe that

I wouldn't be alive today only for Padre Pio. Anything I ever ask him for, I'm never turned down. I fully believe in my own heart that Padre Pio helped me. It's very hard to explain the feeling I have. I know I'm being helped. Even my own children know it. They say here in the house, which is called Villa Pio, 'Oh, Mam was cured by Padre Pio.' They also say at home, 'Oh, Mam prayed for one baby and she got two.' I would give my right hand for Padre Pio.

ELLEN C., CORK, HAS SURVIVED 30 YEARS OF CANCER WITH THE HELP OF PADRE PIO.

My first time ever hearing the name of Padre Pio was in the first year I got married, in 1965. My husband would come in from work and tell me stories of a man he worked with whose sister had been cured by Padre Pio. I would keep asking him, 'Any more news about Padre Pio?' We then had a large picture of him in our apartment. So he was really with us from the start of our marriage.

As the years went on I would hear more about this extraordinary man. But it took until 1977 before I was able to go to Italy to Padre Pio, to see his tomb. He had died in September 1968. I wasn't able to go before that because I wouldn't have had the money. Off I went in July 1977, full of excitement, leaving my husband to take care of our three children. At that time I was 34 years old. When the plane touched down in Italy I almost cried with joy because I was in the country of this great man.

The following year, in July, I had a mastectomy. I was only 35, with a husband and three young children. My whole world came crashing in around me. I pleaded and pleaded with Padre Pio. He wasn't a saint then, although he was my great saint. I pleaded with him to spare me to raise my three children. I had no treatment. I just got on with it because of my three children and I prayed to Padre Pio.

Ten years passed and I was stricken with lung cancer. Padre

Pio was invoked again and again. One day I asked the young doctor, 'Am I going to die?' He answered me by saying, 'You have a few months.' I was in hospital for three weeks at that time and I had to come back for intense chemo over two and a half years of hell. In the meantime I decided to go back to Padre Pio's tomb.

My wonderful husband took me to Italy in January 1988 before the chemo. I was going to Padre Pio to beg for my life. San Giovanni was different compared to the sunny time in July 1977. It seemed cold and lonely to me. We were the only people staying in the hotel by the monastery. The travel agents were great. My husband explained that we had to get there quickly. They got us tickets straight away and gave us a very generous cut in price, which was necessary because we weren't well off.

The tour company gave a letter to the people in the hotel saying I was very ill and would they please take care of me. The hotel got in touch with Father Alessio, who sent for us to come up that night. After a few days we came home tired and with very sore knees. What followed was years of intense treatment, X-rays and blood tests. Padre Pio was invoked every time I drew a breath. I promised him I would be as good a Christian as I could be.

The day came when the doctor told me that I was fine and I would have a check-up once a year. By then I had gone to San Giovanni several times, to Padre Pio. I also went to his mother's and father's grave and I invoked Padre Pio's mother and father to intercede for me to their son. I believe that if you want something badly enough you go to the mother. I wouldn't stop at anything.

Seven years ago I developed a problem with my sternum. I had some treatment for it. I am still praying to Padre Pio because I know he has his hand on my shoulder. One day I told the locum that I was praying to Padre Pio. She said, 'Yes,

I know, it's on your file, Padre Pio helped you.' The doctors had it on the file that Padre Pio did help me.

I was in Rome for the beatification and the canonisation. I think I jumped the highest and clapped the loudest. He is part of our family whether he likes it or not. I should be more grateful than I am, but no matter how grateful I am it will never be enough. I believe from the bottom of my heart that he helped me all along. I don't know what I would have done had Padre Pio never crossed my path. I don't know where I would be now.

JANE SMYTH, COUNTY WICKLOW, RECOVERED FROM A SERIOUS HEART CONDITION.

My devotion began way back in the 1960s when Padre Pio was alive. I was in Holles Street Hospital in 1961 and I had to stay in there for six months waiting for my baby to be born. I had heart trouble because I had rheumatic fever when I was a child. It affected all the valves. I was in bed all the time; they wouldn't let me out of the bed because of my heart. A friend of mine brought me in things of Padre Pio and I prayed to him all the time. I got very devoted to him.

I had the baby, a baby boy, with no problems, but I had to go into Baggot Street in 1963 to have a heart operation. They put a plastic valve in my heart. I was only 24. They told me never to have any more children, that my health was very bad. I prayed to Padre Pio all the time and was greatly devoted to him. Then I was in Holles Street again after that for another baby. I was bad in there again. This lady sent in the Padre Pio glove to me. I blessed myself with the glove and another of my children was born.

After my third child I went into the Mater Hospital for a further heart operation. That was in the late 1970s. They wanted to get at the valve. When they opened me up they discovered that I didn't have the plastic valve at all, it was gone. The heart was grand. They said I had brand-new valves and skin in there. It had healed itself. The doctors and nurses couldn't understand it. The head surgeon came to me and said he couldn't believe it. 'Something happened,' he said, 'you had a wonderful miracle.' They don't know to this day where the plastic valve went.

I went on to have three more children, six overall, and they were all perfect, all fine. I did have to have another operation for my heart when I was bad again in the 1980s or early 1990s. But I really believe that it was devotion and prayer that kept me alive. I believe that what did it was Padre Pio, all the prayer and going to Lourdes as well. I had wonderful cures through him. I think he is marvellous; he is a great man, he is brilliant.

Eventually I got a loan of the glove from the Padre Pio office in Dublin and I blessed a load of people who were very sick. An awful lot of them were healed, completely cured. I also used to send the letters of sick people to San Giovanni and they would put them on Padre Pio's coffin for me. I still pray every single night, every time I think of him, and I bless myself with his relics. I will never forget him for what he did for me.

ROSE, COUNTY KERRY, REFLECTS ON HER DAUGHTER BERNIE'S MIRACULOUS REVIVAL FROM A BRAIN HAEMORRHAGE AND STROKE.

She used to get headaches but the doctor thought it was migraine or chocolate, this thing and that. She was a chemist's assistant but she wanted to study pharmacy in Scotland. So she went over there, to Govan. I think she wasn't feeling that well after going over. She did an exam and didn't do very well and I knew that wasn't Bernie. Then she got a headache and she was in hospital for a few days. She came out and she collapsed. She was in her 30s at the time.

The sensation she got was like a block falling on her head. She had a rented flat. There were children in the flat overhead, the mother was out, but the children rang their mother and an ambulance came straight away. When she went to the hospital one of the nurses said it might be a brain haemorrhage. It was. She was in the hospital in Govan. She had an operation and she got a stroke then. They told her if she bled again, they couldn't do anything for her.

I went over. She was in a bad way. I had photos and she didn't know who was in the photos. It was awful. I wasn't able to sleep, waking up all night saying to myself, 'Will Bernie ever again talk or use her hand or get out of bed?' We met the doctor and he said, 'We're doing our best but we don't know.' I was asking, 'Will she live?' I was saying I didn't mind if she came back in a wheelchair as long as she wouldn't die. He just said they were doing their best for her but they couldn't guarantee that she'd be alright. It was a very worrying time.

I was a long-time devotee of Padre Pio. I kept saying novenas to him. I said novenas so many times that I thought my head would burst. I said them so often that I didn't know what I was saying. I also got the address of a woman called Mrs Davidson, who was elderly and who used to take Padre Pio's glove and relics around to people who weren't well in hospital. She brought the glove into the ward. I wasn't there. Bernie said afterwards that she thought she saw a shadow by the bed; it must have been the woman. She prayed with her and was there for a while.

It was hardly a couple of weeks before she started to walk around. The nurses couldn't believe it when they saw her walking around the ward so quick. We were delighted even though she had all these wires out of her. I had relics and prayers from people and I gave them to her every day. One evening she said every word of the Our Father and I was delighted. She had the haemorrhage on 11 November and she came home on 8 December. She came back to Ireland in an ambulance plane to Farranfore. She only went into hospital for a couple of days because she wanted to come home. She was here with me then for a while.

Initially she didn't know what the teapot was. She'd say, 'Oh, that's something for making the tea.' But, thank God, she got great. It didn't take long for her to recover, only a couple of weeks. She's now working again and is in great form. Eventually the doctor wrote and said that she had made a miraculous recovery. I attribute her recovery to Padre Pio, to him and to the surgeons. She was one of the lucky ones and I have great faith in Padre Pio ever since.

NORA CANTILLON, CORK, REMEMBERS HOW HER SON JONATHAN WAS SAVED BY PADRE PIO.

When Jonathan was a year and a half he inhaled the pines of a fir tree. He came in home to me and he had pines in his mouth. I picked them out and I gave him some water to drink in case he swallowed any, so that he could pass them. My father said to me, 'That's very dangerous.' But we thought no more of it.

A year later he started coughing. He coughed up some blood. We got the doctor and he said, 'That's a blood vessel he broke in his throat while he was coughing.' A few hours later he started coughing again and about a handful of blood came up. That night he started coughing once more. When I looked at Jonathan he was shivery and he looked as though he was dying, he was the colour of death. I got up and I rang the doctor and he said, 'Bring him to hospital immediately.'

I took him to hospital and in the car he was perfect. They checked him out and said, 'He has a very high temperature.' He was in there for about eight or ten days and they said it was a rare pneumonia. So we brought him home. A few months later he started coughing blood again. I took him back in and they said, 'He has a rare blood disease, worse than cancer, he has six months to live and he will become retarded, senile and like a vegetable.'

A few months later he started coughing once again and they said it was an aneurysm in his lung. He had five blood transfusions in five days. They told me I could take him home but he needed surgery, they would do heart and lung surgery on him eventually. I took him to Dublin for this laser treatment they were going to do on him for the aneurysm. It didn't work at all; it was their first failure ever. I said to my husband Brendan, 'Don't worry about it, Padre Pio is with him.' He said, 'Why do you say that?' I said, 'I just know he is.' He opened his wallet and he took out a piece of paper like a little snippet off the top of the *Examiner* and 'Padre Pio' was written on it in biro. He said, 'A young girl gave it to me last night in the pub.' That, to me, was confirmation that he was with him.

I prayed to Padre Pio. I got part of the beard of Padre Pio and had it in my house for about nine days. I had it up in the window with a candle underneath it. I also took Jonathan to a man who had part of the beard of Padre Pio in a little plastic cross. While we were inside waiting, there was a three-dimensional picture up on the wall. One time it was Jesus and then Padre Pio. The next thing, Jonathan looked up at it as the man came in the door and he said, 'Paddy Pio.' When the man heard him saying that he said, 'That child will be alright. Anybody at that age that recognises Padre Pio is one of his spiritual children. He'll be alright.'

I also took him to Mount Melleray; he has a granduncle a priest. I thought, 'Maybe the priest will bless him.' I met this priest and this lady but I never met the granduncle. The priest said, 'What's wrong with him?' I said, 'He's sick.' He said, 'What's wrong?' I said, 'He has an aneurysm in his lung.' The lady said, 'That's strange, my brother had that and Father blessed him and he never had surgery, it was gone.' So Jonathan sat on my lap, Father put his hand on his lung and my hand on his lung and blessed Jonathan and prayed. He said, 'He'll be alright.'

Then we took Jonathan to Dublin for heart and lung surgery. Just as they were going to open him in theatre, they decided they'd go into the lung first. They opened him from the centre of his chest to the centre of his back. The operation took five hours. They removed a third of his lung and what they found was a piece of a fir tree that he had inhaled. When the surgeon came out he said, 'Look, we found something, it looks like a bit of timber.' When he said it, it then registered with me that he had inhaled the pines of a fir tree. I said, 'Oh, I remember.' It never struck me before. He said, 'What?' So I told him. The pines he inhaled had oxygen and moisture and heat in the base of the lung, so they had grown.

He was left home after five days. Once it was gone, he has been perfect since. He is 24 now. I believe it was Padre Pio intervened for him that time. The doctor told me that if the laser treatment had worked it would probably have killed him. But it didn't work. I am sure it was Padre Pio who looked after him and saved him.

MARIE TOONE, COUNTY KERRY, ON HOW PADRE PIO INSPIRED HER CONVERSION BACK TO THE CHURCH WHILE LIVING IN THE UK, WHERE SHE WORKED AS A FASHION INDUSTRY INSIDER AND MASSAGE THERAPIST TO THE STARS.

A friend and I happened to be out partying all the time. We were at every party going. People used to say that we would go to the opening of an envelope. We were always the last to leave the place. People used to joke about it. My twin sister never drank, never smoked and never did anything. She used to spend all-night vigils at a convent. Even though she was in the music industry she would go there, away from the madness of the hectic world, and spend the night in adoration. She used to pray for the conversion of the music industry, the conversion of the entertainment industry and the conversion of her twin sister.

She came back one night with this girl who was Croatian.

I'd been out partying with a whole crowd of people. We'd gone to some big party, drinking quite a bit of champagne and having a great party lifestyle. I came in at about six o'clock in the morning and this girl who I had never even met in my life turned around and said to me, 'This is a terrible time to come home.' There was the smell of alcohol. I was really angry, thinking, 'Who does she think she is?' I'd never met her before. Here she was coming into our house, telling me what to do. I was quite annoyed with her.

She came back another night and she brought me a picture of Padre Pio. I put it up in my room. It was one of those pictures that every time you looked at it you felt he was watching you. Sometimes I'd come in and I'd think, 'Oh, he doesn't look too happy with me tonight.' Sometimes he'd look like he was smiling at you and other times he'd look really cross. I was always drawn to this picture.

Then she brought over a video all about Padre Pio. One night there was a party and I was burnt out. I just thought, 'I don't care if I never see another party again. I'm so tired I'm going to stay in.' I stayed in and I wondered what this video was all about. I put it on. Wow! That was the beginning of the change.

I can't explain it in words but something definitely happened while watching that video, especially during the bit where there's the Consecration of the Mass and he's holding up the Eucharist. Just as he held up the Eucharist something happened within me. I just got goose bumps through my whole body. I started to cry and I could not stop crying. I think I must have cried the whole way through the rest of that video. I knew that Jesus was truly present in that Eucharist. I also could see all the things in my life that weren't right and things that I had to change. That was the beginning of my conversion. I knew I had to change my ways and come back to God. It was all through Padre Pio and I'd never even heard of him.

ALEX QUINN, BELFAST SONGWRITER, EXPLAINS HOW PADRE
PIO'S HELP FOR HIS SON PHILIP INSPIRED HIM TO WRITE A
SONG IN HONOUR OF THE SAINT.

When my son was 15 he was sent home from school with
a sore head, which turned out to be a brain virus. He was
totally paralysed, couldn't walk, couldn't talk, his tongue was
paralysed and he couldn't move at all. We thought we were
going to lose him. A friend of mine told me about a guy who
had the bandage that Padre Pio wore on his side. He had got
the relic from San Giovanni, from the friars there. So he came
down to the Royal Victoria Hospital, he touched my son with
the bandage and we prayed to Padre Pio that we could get a
miracle because we thought he was going to die.

This was about June. He wasn't showing much improvement.
It was thumbs up for 'yes' or thumbs down for 'no'. That was
the only way we could communicate. I would speak and he
would put his thumbs up meaning, 'Yes, I want to go to the
toilet,' or 'I would like a drink.' I'm a schoolteacher and I
was in school. My wife had retired and she was down at the
hospital one day. When I came down to the hospital she told
me that he had spoken his first words. It was 23 September,
the feast of Padre Pio.

From then on he had to learn to speak again and to learn to
walk. His right hand is still a bit paralysed but he passed his
driving test a couple of years ago. He is back walking again,
he is talking. The only worry I have is that he lost all his
friends because he was only 15 and he had to go to a special
unit to learn how to walk and talk again. But this recovery all
started from 23 September.

Then, my wife died three years ago from lung cancer.
I prayed to Padre Pio for her too. She died on the Feast of
the Assumption. She got to Lourdes three weeks before she
died and there was no way she should have been in Lourdes
because she was bedridden. It was a wee miracle in itself that
she actually got to Lourdes. Our Lady looked after her by

letting her die on the Feast of the Assumption. I didn't get the miracle I wanted because I wanted her to live. But I got this vision of my wife going to heaven and that was all part of my dealings with Padre Pio.

I thought, 'Well, Padre Pio has been very good to my family so I'll write a hymn in his honour.' I am a songwriter. I had sung with a group in Belfast called Barnbrack and I wrote a famous song called 'Belfast', which was a big hit. Daniel O'Donnell has recorded 'Belfast' as well; he has done a great version of it. So I sat down with a picture of Padre Pio and I lit one of the Padre Pio candles. I said, 'Tell me what you want me to write.' This is part of the hymn, two verses and the chorus, that came out:

> Let's sing a new song to start each new day,
> Your sins give to Jesus, let him wash them away.
> Ask your little angel to watch over you,
> Send your angel to Padre, he can't refuse you.
>
> St Padre Pio, our saint, our amico,
> We've sent you our angels, they collected our tears.
> St Padre Pio, our saint, our amico,
> Please pass our intentions to the hands of Our Lord.
>
> St Padre Pio, like St Francis had done,
> He suffered the five wounds of God's only son.
> His devotion to Mary was his Rosaries each day,
> To the Sweet Heart of Jesus he always would pray.
>
> St Padre Pio, our saint, our amico,
> We've sent you our angels, they collected our tears.
> St Padre Pio, our saint, our amico,
> Please pass our intentions to the hands of Our Lord.

Then I went over to San Giovanni to deliver the money the record made, which was €10,000. It was a miracle in itself that I got there. I had never gone anywhere without my wife.

I didn't know where I was going. But I got to Rome and I had to get to the bus station to travel the five and a half hours to San Giovanni. Taxi-drivers rip you off in Rome and I got into this taxi and asked the driver to take me to the bus station. As we were talking he asked me, 'Where are you going?' I said, 'San Giovanni.' He was a devotee of Padre Pio so he didn't rip me off. I gave him a wee prayer to Padre Pio and he was delighted. He only charged me €8. When I came back another guy tried to charge me €20 for the same trip. I got the right taxi-driver, a Padre Pio devotee!

I hadn't booked a hotel. I didn't know where I was going or where to get off. It was pitch dark by the time I got to San Giovanni. But halfway through the journey we stopped at this petrol station-cum-shop where you could get a cup of coffee. I was standing at the forecourt of the garage when this wee man came over to me. I think Padre Pio sent him, to be honest. He couldn't speak a word of English and I couldn't speak a word of Italian. But I had an Italian friend and he had written a letter explaining in Italian why I was going to San Giovanni, just in case I got stuck. The letter said I had €10,000 from the sales of the CD which I wanted to give to the friars. I handed him the letter. He read it and I became the prodigal son. He was all over me.

We got back on the bus and he never said anything to me. But I could see him on the mobile phone. What he was doing was booking me into a hotel right beside the friary. He also told me where to get off. I walked behind him for about 20 minutes. He brought me to his house, he opened the garage door, he got me into his car and he drove me up to the hotel. He explained to the manager who I was. Again, I was like the prodigal son. It was a four-star or five-star hotel and I was given one of the best rooms. To this day I don't know his name. I still don't believe it happened to me.

I gave the friars the €10,000. They were delighted. I ended up eating with the friars, which was lovely. They brought me in for my dinner. I sat where Padre Pio had his dinners. I was brought into the wee private church up in the monastery where he said Mass after he wasn't allowed to say Mass in front of anybody. He would just say the Mass on his own there. It was so beautiful. I could feel Padre Pio go through me as I knelt there. That was really special to get in there. There was a real closeness to him.

I got these little signs too from my wife when I was there. There was this staircase leading up to the big, brand-new church which holds thousands. At the foot of the steps something told me to count them. It came into my head, 'Count the steps.' It was like a whispering voice. I counted them and it came to 57. If my wife had been walking up those steps with me that's the age she would have been.

I definitely believe in him and he's still working away for us. I've become a complete devotee of him. My son is fine. He is back studying again. He had to learn to write with his left hand again because his right hand is still paralysed. I go over every year now and go down to the tomb to pray to Padre Pio. For what Padre Pio has done for my son already, for interceding for him, it's great.

MARY DUFF, MOTHER OF INTERNATIONAL SOCCER STAR DAMIEN DUFF, DESCRIBES HOW PADRE PIO HELPED HER FAMILY.

In 1987 Damien's father, Gerard, got himself checked out after burying a brother quite suddenly. He was told he had three months to live. He was 39 and he needed a triple bypass. He didn't smoke in his life and he wasn't overweight. He didn't eat all the rubbish that I would eat. Somebody gave Gerard a Padre Pio relic and that's where it started. He did well and he's still here with us. The lifespan of a bypass is usually eight to ten years. But he's over 20 years now and he hasn't looked back. He hasn't even needed a second one. He developed devotion after that and he swears by Padre Pio.

When Damien went away, his father passed on the relic to him and he has it in his house. Damien is very religious and he has his First Communion Rosary beads hanging on one of the kitchen presses. I'm sure if people walked in they'd think, 'Oh, God.' When he moved from Chelsea I packed all his belongings. The Rosary beads on the kitchen press were packed with all the kitchen stuff. When we went to visit him in Newcastle, there they were again on the kitchen press.

I always prayed to Padre Pio for Damien when he went away to England. About four years after he went to Blackburn he had glandular fever. He had to come home to recuperate because it takes a good while. We brought him over to the Capuchins in Church Street. Gerard and I used to go there once a month to the novena for Padre Pio. This friend of mine borrowed one of the gloves and we left Damien with it. He got well again. There also was a time when Damien had a medal or a relic in his sock or in his boot. He's a good believer. He prays to Padre Pio, which is unusual for a young lad.

A few years ago Damien decided for my birthday that he'd send us to San Giovanni. We were booked there for five days but I have to say I didn't like it. It was wintertime. I couldn't believe the snow. There was definitely three or four feet of snow. There were people on the hill where they have the Stations of the Cross and old women were down on their knees praying in the snow. We didn't have the clothes. Nearly all the hotels were closed for the winter. The one we were in was basic; we were freezing in the bed. The church was beautiful but I ran out of San Giovanni. Gerard loved it although the cold didn't suit him either. He drove in the snow, how I don't know. Obviously, Padre Pio was looking down on us because we got out of there safely.

Since the trip, every two months I get letters from San

Giovanni. I've even got a calendar for the New Year. We put our names down and we've got a diary, the lot. Gerard is still a very good believer and so am I. We all turn to prayer when we need something, don't we? Recently, my young son was doing his driving test and I prayed again to Padre Pio. He passed it.

I go down to the local church maybe two week mornings and say a few prayers for all the family. I also have a Padre Pio medal, with a red piece of cloth in it, in my purse. Every time I change my purse the medal gets moved as well. Gerard still brings a Padre Pio relic in his wallet everywhere he goes. Certainly, Padre Pio is a dominant figure in our family. I've got loads of favours from him over the years. He just seems to have been in our lives since 1987.

GEMMA DILLON, COUNTY MEATH, REVEALS THE STRANGE ROLE OF PADRE PIO IN A DEVASTATING EVENT THAT OCCURRED IN 1983.

We have a friend, Father Augustine McGregor, who is in Mellifont Abbey. He has written extensively on the life of Padre Pio, particularly the early years. He is a Cistercian. Back in 1983 he had a lot of notes loosely transcribed from Italian into poor English. He asked me would I tidy things up and put the notes into better English because he wanted to use them in his book. I agreed to do this but he said, 'Be careful because something has happened to everybody who has ever done anything with these before, and you are the third person to have them.' I said, 'That's nonsense, of course I will do it.'

He was in our house on the afternoon of 22 September 1983. He was having dinner and we went over a couple of things. Then he went away. I was going to bed a bit early so I said I would take the stuff up with me and start it up in bed. I started marking the first couple of pages. Eddie came to bed later. I had put the pages out on the floor beside me. At a quarter past two that morning I woke up and I had this most intense sense of fear and fright, a feeling that something terrible was going to happen. It was a dreadful sense of evil that I've never experienced before or since. The hair literally stood up on my head. I woke Eddie up and said, 'There is something going to happen.' He got up and looked from room to room and saw nothing. He looked outside and there was nothing there. He said, 'You just had a bad dream, go back to sleep.'

At half past two on the morning of 23 September, which was exactly the time and date that Padre Pio had died 15 years earlier, we had a vicious raid in our home and seven raiders broke in. It was the time when some group of Republicans were doing their business, rampaging around the country. They shot our dog. They shot Eddie and left him lying on the floor. He put his hands up against our bedroom door and they shot through the door. Two bullets went through his liver. He lost his spleen and part of his pancreas, the bottom of his lung and stomach. He has been invalided ever since.

I was hurt as well, pushed around badly and I injured my neck and my knee and had to have a lot of surgery, with a knee joint replaced and so on. They stole our money. Eddie wasn't expected to live. For the following two months he was fighting for his life. Father Alessio was visiting Ireland at the time. The next day he came down to visit Eddie and he whispered to Eddie that he was going to live. He said, 'You will live, Padre Pio told me so.' Unfortunately, he forgot to tell me and we had many months of stress. We never expected to survive it and nobody expected Eddie to live. He had a two per cent chance of survival but he somehow got through it and he is still up and running.

About seven or eight months later we went back out to San Giovanni in thanksgiving. I was in a neck brace. Eddie was wearing a bag on his back because the wounds were weeping all the time and the medicine couldn't get them to close. They had to be dressed twice a day. We decided to rest up in Rome for a couple of days. I dressed them there and they were weeping. We then travelled to San Giovanni by train, having dressed the weeping wounds just before we left Rome. We took the bus from Foggia up to San Giovanni Rotondo. When we arrived it was time for dinner. Eddie said, 'You had better dress the wounds before dinner or else they will leak through my shirt.' When I took the bag off his back the wounds had completely closed. They had totally healed and never opened again.

In San Giovanni they were hugely interested in the fact that the shooting happened at exactly the same moment as Padre Pio's death, on the night I was editing the notes. Having been warned by Father Augustine that things had happened to other people was also odd. Apparently, the house of one person went on fire and she gave the notes back. Then I had them and we had the raid. That my husband survived was some miracle. That Father Alessio was in Dublin at the time was odd too. It was all strange, to say the least.

JOSEPH LACEY, DUBLIN, ON HIS RECOVERY FROM CANCER.
Twenty-one years ago, when I was fifty, I wasn't too well and I was out of work for about a week. I was exhausted and I didn't know what was wrong. In the midst of that week a religious magazine was dropped in through the hall door. I read the magazine and I came across an article in it about Padre Pio. This chap who was an atheist had met him and he got the scent of roses. He was very impressed by Padre Pio. I thought the story was interesting.

I went back to work. One evening I was out in the back garden and a neighbour of mine came down to talk to me. He said, 'Joe, have you got a sore eye?' I said, 'Well, if I have I don't know about it.' My wife had a look and said, 'I don't see anything wrong.' That happened around September but by Christmas I definitely had a sore eye. It was running water and starting to get a little bit red.

I went to my GP and I went twice to a hospital and they thought it was an eye infection. They told me to use an ointment. It didn't get better. I went into the hospital again after Christmas so that I'd be fine for work. Two doctors said they thought it was alright. However, one doctor said, 'On your way out go in to the specialist and let him have a look at the X-rays.' He looked at them as I was sitting there. He and a colleague were pointing to things on the X-rays. I said, 'Oh, dear.' He said, 'You have a tumour. It's not urgent but if we don't do something about it you'll lose your eye.'

They scheduled me for a scan at the end of that week in another hospital. I went in for the scan on the Friday. When I went in the guy that was in charge said, 'You must be an emergency because if it wasn't an emergency you wouldn't be here now.' After the scan I was called in for a biopsy. The results came back and it was confirmed that I had cancer. They said that the problem had existed for approximately 12 months. An operation was scheduled.

As I left the hospital a lay sister that I had been speaking to handed my wife a prayer to Padre Pio. She said, 'That's the only thing that's going to save your husband.' That was on a Friday. The house was packed with people on the Saturday and the Sunday, on the basis that I was going to die. That weekend one of the family came up and brought with him a small cardboard box with a little window on the front. In it was a little box of water containing the bud of a rose. I was in bed at this stage. My wife brought it up to me. On the Monday my nephew got the mitten of Padre Pio and I was blessed with it.

They then brought me in for the operation and I lost my eye. Given the option that faced me it wasn't as big a problem as a person might think. The option I had was that I was going to have a cauliflower growing out of the side of my head if I didn't have the operation. So I had the operation followed by radiotherapy. Subsequently, the rosebud that was sitting in the water on the cabinet opened out into a full-blown rose. It's on a shelf now in the living-room, crimson red, sitting in a little plastic container 21 years later.

After a couple of months I returned to work. A year later I saw a lump on the side of my face adjacent to where my eye was removed. I had surgery and the hospital confirmed it was malignant. Glands had become contaminated. Another eighteen months or two years later I started to develop more glands down the side of my face, to the left of my chin. There were several lumps starting to form. Once again, I was operated on. They removed a whole line of glands all the way down to my chest. They said, 'If we hadn't done that you would have ended up with lung cancer.' That was major surgery.

Ever since then I've been fine. I've had a fantastic life. I have travelled so much. As of now, I have the best vision in the house. But the interesting thing was that every time I got bad news something associated with Padre Pio, however trivial, would come my way. It might even be a key-ring with his picture, or something like that.

Those who don't want to believe will say it's coincidence. But I have no doubt whatsoever. As far as I'm concerned, it's intervention from heaven. I think the power of prayer is extraordinary. I had prayed to Padre Pio every day and I still do. He was everywhere and I know he helped me.

EILEEN O'DONNELL, COUNTY KERRY, EXPLAINS HOW PADRE PIO HELPED HER SON.
My son was attending college as a mature student and he was going back to do his third year when he had an accident. He was going to work one morning and he was in the back of a car when they had a crash. He was one-twentieth of an inch from being paralysed. The consultant said to me, 'Oh, he was lucky.' I said, 'What do you mean?' He said, 'Come over here and I'll show you.' He showed me the scan. He said, 'If

that was just one-twentieth of an inch nearer, his spinal cord would have been severed and he would have been paralysed for life.'

He was on the flat of his back before going back to his studies. He was in severe pain. Then he went into college. But he could only lie flat or stand up, he couldn't sit. The first day back he came home and he had ferocious pain. He couldn't go to lectures because he couldn't sit down. He took painkillers. The following morning he said, 'Mum, I won't be able to make it.' I thought he was going to be out for a year. I knew that if he missed out the year in college he wouldn't have gone back and finished his degree.

We have an oratory a few miles over the road from us. I was going to Mass and I picked up this older lady. I said to her, 'Will you say a prayer for him because I don't think he's going to make college this year.' She said, 'Have you devotion to Padre Pio?' I said, 'I haven't.' She said, 'His feast day will be in three days' time and when we come home I'll give you a small little relic and a novena prayer and do the three-day novena to Padre Pio.'

On the way home she said, 'Come in and I'll give you the relic and the novena prayer.' The relic was just a small little plastic one with the stigmata on the hands on the front of it and some cloth. The cloth had probably been rubbed onto something of Padre Pio's. So I got the relic and novena prayer and came home.

When I got home he was asleep. He was about six weeks in pain at this stage. I rubbed the relic to him without waking him. He didn't know it happened at all. About three hours later he got up and he said, 'Will you drive me to college?' At that stage I said, 'No, I won't because you're only going to do more damage.' He said, 'No, I feel I'm better.' I said, 'Alright, but you'll be sorry.' He went into college that day and he never looked back.

It was instant. At the time I didn't have devotion to Padre Pio but I have devotion now. When my son went back to the consultant everything was cured, it had healed. It probably would have healed eventually but not in time to get him back to college. A month later he couldn't have gone back to finish his degree.

We pray for a lot of things but we don't always get answers the way we want them. But that certainly was an answer. It has opened my eyes about Padre Pio. It was miraculous really, it was an instant miracle. I now pray to Padre Pio every day. I believe it was his intercession that cured my son, there's no two ways about it.

BRIGID McCAFFREY, COUNTY MONAGHAN, RECOVERED FROM MULTIPLE SCLEROSIS.

Around 1990 I got multiple sclerosis. They had difficulty diagnosing me at the beginning. I suppose I wasn't diagnosed properly until about 1995. I didn't really know what was wrong with me. I had very little energy. My left eye was always very painful. My vision wasn't impaired but I had terrible headaches. I had pins and needles on the left side of my body. I was put on medication.

I would have heard of Padre Pio in *The Irish Catholic* going way back to the 1960s. We would buy *The Irish Catholic* and there was an old man down the road who would read about Padre Pio. He was a great man for reading and I would hear about Padre Pio from him. Other than that, I wouldn't have had any connection as such. The first time I really had a connection was when I had my daughter. I went, by chance, to a priest who was a Capuchin. My devotion really started there.

I went to Rome for the beatification of Padre Pio. It was just by chance that the trip came up. My mother was living at the time and I was minding her. A friend rang me to say there was a ticket available to Rome, to attend the beatification. I said, 'Oh, gosh, there's no way I can go because I'm looking after my mother.' I was also working and my daughter was young. So I said, 'No.'

My mother died in February 1999. She died on a Sunday and on the Monday morning this person rang again and said, 'I've still got this ticket, would you be interested in going?' I said, 'My mother has passed away so I can go now.' It was like I was meant to go. So I went and I enjoyed it very much. I put out my heart in prayers to Padre Pio. I also went to San Giovanni. I prayed at his tomb. I also went to his Confessional box and to his cell. It meant a lot to me.

I noticed a change after I came home. The pain in my left eye was very much relieved as a result of going to Rome. I was better in every way. I had more energy. I felt like I was on the winning side. I then went a second time, for the canonisation. I said, 'I'm definitely not going to miss the canonisation.' When it came along I went. It was an electric event. It was a very deserving event for such a holy man and a man of our times. I went back to San Giovanni again. After that, my eye completely cleared up. I was even better still.

I've never looked back. I have a very close connection with Padre Pio ever since. His statue is on my fireplace. He's looking down on me in my kitchen. But I should have more devotion than I have. I still take my medication. I keep getting my injections. I had been off them but the nurse comes out here once a year and she said, 'In case that comes back, take them. You know how you were originally. I can't force you to go back on them but I'd rather you did.' So I did.

I'm great now. I'm working two jobs. I work hard. The symptoms are gone. The pins and needles are gone. I should be going back to my neurologist in Dublin but I haven't attended her in five years. Considering what multiple sclerosis is, I've been extraordinarily lucky. I really believe it was Padre Pio who saw me through. I have no doubts about that. He listened to me and it had to be through him that I now feel so good. He's the first man I think of when I'm in trouble of any sort.

LIAM COYLE, FORMER DERRY CITY FOOTBALLER, ON HIS CAREER-THREATENING INJURY.

I got an injury playing for Derry City down in Dundalk in 1989. I was only 21 at the time. The injury turned out to be an athletic condition, not really an injury as such. The bone was wasting away in my knee and there was a hole in my bone. Bits of bone were breaking off. The hole was getting bigger and bigger. I was told I was going to have to stop because I would have ended up in a wheelchair by the time I was 30 if I kept playing.

We had played Benfica at the Brandywell three days before I got hurt. Sven Goran Eriksson, who was the manager at the time, was interested in taking me to Benfica. Manchester United, Celtic and even Paris Saint-Germain were interested as well. At that time there was a lot of talk about me going here, there and everywhere. Because of the injury it never materialised. I went to New York and Chicago and Paris and Germany and London, everywhere, and every doctor in the world told me the same thing. There was really no way I was ever going to play again. It just shows how wrong doctors can be.

My mother was the one that prayed to Padre Pio and got the mitts. She had prayed to him all the time. This is going back all the way to the early 1980s when her friend died of cancer, from that time on. She had medals everywhere. She used to have medals in my bag going to play games. She used to have medals in my boots. Whenever she got his mitt here I used to have to go and get a rub of it. That was even before the injury.

After the injury my mother just kept praying. Every avenue was explored. There was a lady in Derry, a very holy woman, who was called Betty Beales. She is supposed to have seen a vision of Padre Pio. I was sent up to see Betty around 1990. There were hundreds, thousands of people going to see her. She just prayed with me and put her hands on me and told me that Padre Pio was looking after me because my mother had prayed to him for so long. She told me that I would be alright. From the minute I went to see her I never had another bit of bother with it.

Two years after I had stopped playing I was back playing football again. Since then I've won the league twice, I've won three cup medals, I've won player of the year awards, I've played for the League of Ireland. For the injury I had, I have had a pretty decent career. And Padre Pio has had a very big role to play in that.

Don't get me wrong, I'm a Catholic but I don't ram it down anyone's throat. There are lots of sceptics out there but for me at the time it was a big help because not only was I dealing with an injury that was keeping me from playing but mentally I was going through a bad time. I was drinking a bit too heavily because I wasn't playing football. There's a lot of people had a lot of faith and I think it just helped me in some way.

My mother is dead now but she had a great belief. She had great faith in Padre Pio and he always looked after her. I do believe that all her praying, and all her faith that she showed in me, helped me. I am married now, with kids, and I've never been happier. I think that's all to do with what went on at that time. Padre Pio had a big role to play. I would love to go to Italy. My mother never went there because she was afraid of flying. But I would just love to go and experience it and see where everything is.

I've also never forgotten Betty Beales. She wouldn't take money off me but she said to me once, 'At some stage you will acknowledge me.' I'll never forget that when I won the player of the year award in Dublin I went up and I said, 'I just want to mention a woman who had a lot of faith in me and her name is Betty Beales.' She knows what she did for me.

DUBLIN RESIDENT ROSALYN O'MAHONEY RECOUNTS HOW HER FATHER, KERRYMAN JACK McCARTHY'S LEG WAS SAVED THROUGH PADRE PIO'S INTERCESSION.

Daddy was in his early to mid-70s and had severe artery disease. The main artery to his leg was blocked. He went to his doctor in Dublin and he decided that he would operate. I was outside the operating theatre. After about two hours there was nothing happening and the doctor wasn't coming out. I decided to call a nurse to ask the theatre sister what was going on. About an hour and a half later the doctor appeared after three and a half hours of surgery. He appeared in his green overalls to say that he was just lucky to be able to finish the operation. He didn't have any positive news on Daddy's leg and he'd discuss it tomorrow.

The following day I met the doctor and he said he wanted 24 hours to see how the leg was coming along. He eventually called me and said that he thought he'd have to amputate, that there was actually no life in the leg. We looked at the leg and it was all white, like an ice block and it had brown spots on it. 'To be honest with you, I'd rather die,' my father said. 'I don't know if I'll let them take me down to theatre.' I said, 'Well, you can't keep your leg like this because there's no blood supply to it.'

I had an old friend and she had a Padre Pio mitten. Mammy and I went to her house that afternoon and got the mitten. It was very, very special at the time having this. I went into the hospital again. I went to Daddy with the mitten and he caught it in his hand and he kissed it. He said prayers and he rubbed it profusely up and down his leg. He kissed the mitten again. I thought to myself, 'My God, what belief and what faith!'

After a few minutes I took the mitten and I went next door where there were two friends of Daddy's in another ward.

One had a little bit of faith and the other had absolutely no belief whatsoever. The first took it and the other took it but he had no belief. The disbelieving guy wanted to go home for Christmas and I said, 'You'll never get home for not believing, I'll bring you something else tomorrow, a relic I have at home. But I'll only give it to you on one condition – that you believe – because Padre Pio won't do anything unless you believe in him.' So I gave it to him the next day and he made it home for Christmas and lived for another two years.

The following day they took Daddy down to theatre and he came back up with his leg. There was five per cent blood flow to his leg. By the end of the day it was ten per cent and all the following week there was a ten per cent trickle of blood. They had found a trickle, it saved his leg and it was a miracle.

He still has his leg. He had his toe removed since, but it was just amazing. He believes that it was Padre Pio saved his leg. I also absolutely believe that Padre Pio is a miracle man. It is definitely through the power of prayer that Daddy is still alive. And I do believe that it was a miracle that his leg was saved.

ANGELO PERMA, COUNTY OFFALY, TOGETHER WITH HIS BROTHER ANTONIO SURVIVED A HORRIFIC CAR CRASH AND ERECTED A STATUE OF PADRE PIO IN THE CHURCH IN BANAGHER.

In 1979 myself and Antonio and a friend of ours had a very, very bad accident. We were in a car and a truck came straight and hit us. I only remember a big boom and we were in hospital. The car was destroyed. It was absolutely smashed. They had to cut out the doors of the car. In fact, when my father and the other chap's father passed where we had the crash and saw the car they said, 'What are we going to find in hospital now?' They thought there could be three coffins waiting for them.

The three of us were very, very lucky to survive. The driver had a very bad leg and nine or ten stitches up in his eyes. My brother got a few stitches. I had a bang on the legs and under the neck. We were confused, we didn't know what happened. Dad was going around very sad because he said, 'I could have lost two sons.' We thought what happened was a miracle. We realised that there is something up there, absolutely. After that we always said that some day we would have to do something.

We believe that Padre Pio had a role to play in our survival. We believe we were being looked after. Where we lived in Italy is about two and a half hours from San Giovanni so we always prayed to him. Almost every year now we go to Padre Pio's place. We go home for two or three weeks and we take a day or a day and a half and go to San Giovanni. When we go to bed at night, before we go to sleep we say some prayers to Padre Pio.

We got a statue in December 2005 and we put it up in Banagher, outside the church. We got the statue in Italy from a man that was doing the statues. In Banagher, people go down and see it. They put roses, now and again, and bunches of flowers at the statue. They are very, very good. We always said that some day we would have to do something for being alive. And this is it.

EILEEN REA, CORK, HAS A GRANDSON WHO ATTAINED PERFECT HEALTH FOLLOWING THE INTERVENTION OF PADRE PIO.

I have a grandson in the States and when he was small his mother was told that he would hardly be able to walk because he had a lot of arthritis in the legs. His knees were all swollen out from it and he was really very bad. My daughter brought him home here because he was very fragile and she wanted a second opinion in Ireland. When he was home I rubbed him all over with the relic of Padre Pio. The following morning he woke up and he called me, not his mum, to pick him up out of the bed. He couldn't come down the stairs on his own as he was only a year and a half. He pointed to the door and he pointed to the relic. He wanted to be rubbed all over again.

He went back to the States after their visit and went back to the doctor. 'I don't know what happened,' the doctor said, 'but you must have a friend in heaven. The arthritis has disappeared.' My daughter said to the doctor, 'It's not my prayers but Mum has a great friend in heaven, Padre Pio.' Years later my grandson represented the States in soccer at Under-16 level. They went to Peru and he played for them there. I have no doubt whatsoever that it was Padre Pio was responsible.

MARIE TOONE, COUNTY KERRY, WITH THE STORY OF HER MIRACULOUS ROSARY BEADS.

I was at the Shrine of Our Lady of Walsingham, in England, and I was in the little Slipper Chapel there when all of a sudden this priest breezes in and announces that he is about to say Mass, would we join him? I looked around and there was only one other person there. I thought, 'We can't leave him to say Mass on his own.' It turned out that this priest was called Father Joseph Pius Martin and he was the priest that had to go and gather all of the other friars when Padre Pio was dying and tell them to come quickly to his room. We spent the whole afternoon with him and the stories he told were all about Padre Pio.

Before we went our separate ways I took out a beautiful set of crystal Rosary beads that I had bought in my local church. He took them and he tucked them into the bloodstained mitten that the Padre had been wearing up until he died. He blessed them. A few months after that, I was in Aylesford at a Youth 2000 gathering and I was invited to meet Father Slavco, who was the spiritual director to the visionaries in Medjugorje. He invited us to come into a tiny little side chapel in the priory where Ivan Dragicevic, the visionary, was going to have an apparition. I had the Rosary beads in my hand. After the apparition Ivan looked at me and he said, 'The Blessed Mother kissed your Rosary beads.' So my beads became the most precious things I ever possessed. I thought, 'I am never parting with them.'

Later, I was at Padre Pio's beatification at the Vatican. The day before the beatification I decided to go to Confession. I was waiting in the queue for Confession when three American ladies approached and asked were there any English-speaking priests for Confession. I had the beads in my hand because I wanted Pope John Paul II's blessing on them. This American lady said to me, 'Oh, my God, your beads are beautiful.' I said, 'Thank you, thank you.'

While she was in the Confessional I heard an inner voice telling me to give my beautiful beads to this American that I've never met before in my life. She didn't know anything about the story of them. I was broken-hearted but I knew I would have no peace if I didn't do it. So I gave her the beads and she started to cry. I said, 'You might as well know the story behind them.' So I told her. When I told her she was sobbing.

I also told her the story of how we'd been in our local church and there was a whole family and they were all crying their eyes out. The son had been critically injured in an accident. He had been working when a crane came on top of him and crushed his skull. He was in intensive care, on life support. They weren't holding out any hope. I asked the father, mother and sister would they like to borrow my Rosary beads and take them and lay them under his pillow. Within hours of the beads being under the pillow he made a full and miraculous recovery. So I gave her the beads. Her name was Colleen. We exchanged numbers and we never met again during that trip.

A couple of years passed and the phone rang. I picked up the phone and it's an American accent, 'Hello, is that Marie?'

I said, 'Yes.' 'I don't know if I've got the right number,' she said, 'are you the Marie that gave this strange American lady the most beautiful beads in the Vatican?' I said, 'Yes.' She went, 'Oh, my God. I have been trying to reach you all this time. You can't imagine the miracles caused by these beads. They have been around schools, prisons, hospitals. They've been venerated by thousands. I've wanted to tell you for so long but I couldn't find your number anywhere. My friend who was with me at the Vatican said, "Pray to Padre Pio, he'll find the number. After all, it was at his beatification that you met." No sooner had I started praying when your number fell out of a book.' And that was the cause of her phoning me.

'I have something else to tell you,' she said. 'I'm dying, I have an inoperable brain tumour and I'm in a wheelchair. I don't know how long I've got because the tumour is situated right next to the pituitary gland and it's on top of a major blood vessel. They cannot biopsy because it's far too dangerous due to the location of the tumour.' She had a lot of other problems as well. She was seeing five top neurosurgeons at the Mayo Clinic and basically they told her, 'There's nothing we can do for you, go do what you're going to do because you're going to die.' She said to me, 'I have a dying wish and it's to go to Medjugorje and to see you again. Do you think you could make the trip?' I said, 'I'd love to make the trip.'

Cutting a long story short, I arrived in Medjugorje and found that Colleen was there already, she had been healed and she was out of the wheelchair. She'd been cured of the brain tumour. Apparently, they had taken Colleen in a wheelchair to where the visionary Vicka was giving a talk. All the crowds were there. She couldn't move, she was in agony, she was in a wheelchair. She had her head down and she was praying, 'Holy Mother, if only Vicka could come and just put her hands on my head. I would know then that you were really listening to me and that it was you yourself that had really touched my head.' Apparently, it was like the parting of the Red Sea. The crowds just pulled aside and Vicka came straight for her and laid her hands on her. She felt a burning heat go down through her body. Later, when she went to Mass, she got out of her wheelchair to the astonishment of everyone who was with her.

While we were in Medjugorje she still had the Rosary beads and she would not let the Rosary beads out of her hands. She then turned around to me and started crying and said that her husband said she had to give me the beads. So she gave me back the beads in Medjugorje. I now have the beads back in my possession. I have been going around speaking and I have the Rosary beads with me. The amount of people that queue up and want to hold the beads! I've had letters from people. One woman who has scoliosis of the spine, who is from Canada and who prayed with the beads, she wrote to me from Canada saying she had got back, seen the physiotherapists and they couldn't believe that she was the same person.

The real miracles are the conversions of hearts and souls. People say to me that when they hold the beads it's like an electric sensation on the skin. People start crying as they are holding them. They can't stop crying. So many people have prayed the whole Rosary on them. Marija, the visionary, has prayed the whole Rosary on them. The Bishop of Amsterdam has prayed with them. It's quite amazing the people who have prayed on the Rosary beads. So the story of the Rosary continues. And it's all down to Padre Pio. The story blows my mind away to this day.

FATHER GERARD COLEMAN, COUNTY CORK, DETAILS HIS RECOVERY FROM A MYSTERIOUS VIRUS.

I was 19 at the time when I contracted this virus. It was very close to Weil's disease and there was nothing they could do for it. I couldn't eat or drink. I couldn't put anything down or it would come straight up again. All I could do was take water. All the muscles were wasting away. The infection was eating through me. They couldn't even give me a drip, for some reason. There was absolutely nothing they could do; they were only observing although they couldn't have been more professional and helpful.

I had a high temperature of 104 and I had only a sheet over me. I had lumbar punctures and all sorts of things. There were Mass cards all around the bed. I was that way for three weeks and I was six weeks altogether in hospital, in intensive care. They were doing nothing for me although they were in and out to me. I don't think they ever figured out what was wrong. It was looking grim.

After three weeks, one night one of the boys came in with the glove of Padre Pio. It was my mother asked for it to come in. I remember it arriving. It was placed on me, on my forehead. The person prayed with me with the mitten. The next morning my uncle came down and said, 'Will you try to eat a bit today?' I hadn't intended taking anything. But when he mentioned it I said, 'I will.' I hadn't eaten for three weeks. Once I got back on the food I was on the mend. Three weeks later I was out of hospital.

I was up in time to see the Pope's visit, which was in 1979. I went to Galway. That was about three months after. I slowly came around again and had to build up my body. My parents would put it down to Padre Pio. I had known nothing of Padre Pio at the time. I thought it was my own health pulled me through. I knew there was God in it and prayers and Masses. But I can really say that it was after the night of the glove that I got up and I was flying.

It was many years later that I went to San Giovanni. I was a priest by then, having gone into a seminary when I was 28. It was the year of the death of the Pope. It coincides with the fact that I went to see him the year he came to Ireland, which was just after I got sick. I passed down through Rome and on to San Giovanni. I find it strange in a way. I think the Pope had something to do with it too. There was a connection between them. They had met each other and he had beatified him. He had great time for Padre Pio.

I was leading a group to San Giovanni that time. I was very lucky to get special time with Padre Pio at his tomb. I was sitting one night in the oratory. Suddenly, this door opened and I just walked in. I had said Mass there a few times and I knew the run of the sacristy. There's a kind of a lift down into the chamber where he is. I was in there for about an hour and a half on my own at the tomb. I only intended to go down and be outside the cage. But the whole cage was open and there was nobody down there, only me. It was like, 'Come in, this is what you've come for.' I said to myself, 'This is unbelievable.'

The monks themselves came in to pray and I was there with my head down on the tomb. They all gathered around. I got up to let them at it. They spoke in Italian and they just signalled for me to stay as they did the Divine Office that night. I couldn't believe it. I would definitely say that Padre Pio had something to do with my recovery although it took a long reflection for me to come around to that view. I certainly believe in him now.

NUALA BRADY, FORMER ITALIAN PILGRIMAGE MANAGER FOR JOE WALSH TOURS, DESCRIBES SOME OF THE MIRACLES SHE ENCOUNTERED THROUGH HER JOB.

Members of groups would tell you their stories. One woman had a sick daughter; she only had three valves in her heart. She was only about four or five. The doctor said, 'She can't live on three valves, she's going to die.' The mother heard about Padre Pio and she was given a Padre Pio magazine. She brought it home and looked through it. That night, or the next night, the daughter started screaming in the bed, 'There's a man in the room, there's a man in the room.' They were trying to calm her down saying, 'There isn't, you're fine.'

Later on, the daughter said, 'Oh, I've found the man; he's here in the sitting-room.' They went into the sitting-room to see who she was talking about. They looked down and on the couch was the magazine with a picture of Padre Pio. She then arranged to go to hospital. The doctor took an X-ray and she had *four* valves in her heart, not three! I met the girl on the coach and she was then 21.

Another time, I rang an old lady who was involved with the Padre Pio groups. I would never do that. I wasn't asking her about a group or whether she was going over to San Giovanni. I just wondered would I ring her or not. Next thing, I heard this crumbling as the phone dropped. She said something like 'help' or whatever. I thought, 'What's that?' The phone was then off the hook and I thought, 'She has obviously fallen and she needs help.' I knew there was something wrong.

I rang directory enquiries and I got the neighbour next door. I telephoned the neighbour and said, 'Would you go in straight away as she has fallen or something.' It turned out that she had fallen out of bed the night before and she was praying for somebody to ring her. She couldn't understand why I rang her. It was uncanny. She felt it was Padre Pio because there was no reason for me to phone her. I just did.

There were strange things that would happen to me too. Say I had a group going out and there were people who wanted to go and I hadn't room for them. I remember, at one stage, there were 39 people on a waiting-list. I said at home, 'I'm going to pray to Padre Pio that I need 39 extra seats because I don't want to let anyone down.' That exact number cancelled or changed. I got it to the last one. It was so uncanny. I might be looking for a hotel and it would work out. That sort of thing happened all the time.

Before I got to San Giovanni I thought, 'What is all this about?' When I got there I asked for something which I put on a list and put in the petition box. I wrote a huge, big list and put it into the box to see what would happen. And something did happen, the worry was taken away. Padre Pio's motto was, 'Pray, hope and don't worry.' I was an awful worrier but it just went. I had a great belief in him then. That's why I enjoyed doing it so much.

ALICE DE LA COUR, COUNTY CORK, REFLECTS ON HER MOTHER NORA'S DEATH FROM CANCER AT THE AGE OF 80, ON CHRISTMAS DAY 2005.

On one of the evenings that I was taking care of my mother, she got a little bit of a fright with her breathing. She got into breathing difficulties. She was very uncomfortable. I looked at her chest and she was covered in red marks. I said, 'Mam, maybe you have a little chest infection, maybe we should call somebody.' I called the doctor, the young locum came and she said, 'Oh, Mrs de la Cour, your chest is looking really inflamed. You have a lot of little red marks.' She gave her something for it.

Next morning, which was Christmas Eve, we were chatting about it. Suddenly there was a great laugh in the kitchen. It turned out that all the red marks had come from a Padre Pio Rosary beads that she had. The dye had come off the Rosary beads. She had the beads and a relic of Padre Pio on her chest. She kept them there all the time. She had a great laugh because of it.

What she believed was that her faith in Padre Pio was so good that she didn't have any pain whatsoever, that he looked after her all the time. She swore by that until she went to sleep that night. She never woke up after that. The following morning she was unconscious. She was in her transition, in another place between unconscious and dying. She was that way for hours and hours and hours. She had believed from the minute she was diagnosed that Padre Pio would look after her. It was fantastic to have the faith that she had. She died with a smile on her face because of her belief in him.

PAULINE, COUNTY CLARE, HAS A HUSBAND TONY WHO RECOVERED FROM CANCER.

In October 1999 Tony wasn't feeling very well. He was around 59 years old. He had an awful pain in his tummy. He was losing weight and he was putting it down to an ulcer. He went to the doctor and had some X-rays and a colonoscopy. They told him he had cancer of the colon. He had to be operated on straight away.

He was really ill after the operation. They were giving him chemo. He improved a little bit but then he went back down again. He was sent home and his doctor was coming every morning and every evening and during the night. He was picking up infections very easily. He was down to about five and a half stone. He wasn't eating at all, not even a dry biscuit. Basically, the doctors said, 'There is no more we can do.'

The priest was coming every night and he was anointed and everything. The hospice nurses were here day and night. Tony doesn't realise half of it because he was so out of it with the morphine. He was on an awful lot of medication. The bones were out through him and his clothes were falling off him. His GP called me into the sitting-room and said, 'Pauline, there's no more we can do, this is it.'

One evening Tony's boss came with some dried rose petals of Padre Pio in an envelope. They came from the tomb. He said, 'Put them under Tony's pillow, they have worked for a lot of people that I've spoken to over the years.' Of course, we did anything that might help. The next thing they started giving him more chemo and Tony just turned around. That was the turning-point. It was unbelievable. I asked his doctor about it and he said, 'There's no explanation, it's unbelievable.'

Our daughter was getting married shortly afterwards, in 2000, and everything was arranged. She was coming from London. Tony gave a speech and was up dancing. Tony's doctor attended the wedding as well. A lot of people were asking about Tony and how he was so well. The doctor said,

'This is unbelievable, I'm sitting at a table where there are 12 people and they're all saying the same thing, "How come?" But I can't explain it.' He had once told me that Tony had roughly nine days to live.

Tony just took it from there. He started eating and going out walking. He went out for a pint. The weight slowly started to come back on. He returned to work as well. They couldn't believe it that he worked for another five years after all the chemo, radiation and everything. Tony is now like a teenager. He is 66 and he looks very well. The cancer is all gone, gone completely, thank God. There's no explanation for it. His doctor often shakes his head and says, 'I can't believe it.'

Tony has great faith in Padre Pio. Padre Pio was a great favourite even before he got sick, the devotion was always there. He goes to his Mass once a month. He prays to him all the time. I also believe it was Padre Pio. I pray to him myself. We have Padre Pio in the car. I think he was a great man and I believe he has intervened in a lot of things for a lot of people. Tony does as well. Padre Pio is his man, and that's it.

ELISA MUSCEDERE, THE ITALIAN PROPRIETOR OF LISA'S TRATTORIA IN DUBLIN, CLAIMS HER FAMILY IS PROTECTED BY PADRE PIO.

My devotion to Padre Pio began when my son was dying. My son, at the age of two months, received eight bypasses to the brain and to the heart. It was life and death. The only saint I was praying to was Padre Pio. My son is now 27 and he has the health of a bull. My daughter had an accident when she was fifteen and a half. She was hit by a hit-and-run driver. They only gave her 24 hours to live. She had a fractured skull and she nearly lost her leg. I begged Padre Pio to release her from the dead. She is now alive and she is 35.

It's miraculous the way Padre Pio works. Anything I ask for he gives to me. My house is full of Padre Pio. I have a shrine to him, down through the hall. There's the Madonna, Jesus,

St Francis and the statue of Padre Pio. I have a picture in the restaurant. I have a cross in my restaurant. I have a Pope John Paul II photograph. I have all the saints. But I specially have Padre Pio.

I pray to him every day. I say the Rosary every day. I was studying to become a nun but my mother said, 'No.' In those days there was family to support and my mother said I had to go to work because my father died. I talk to Padre Pio when I go to bed at six o'clock in the morning, because we work very late. I say, 'Goodbye, Padre Pio, I will see you tomorrow.' He also sends his perfume to me. It's of flowers, and when there are no flowers around I know it's him. That might happen three or four times in a year.

He comes in my dreams as well. He comes when I need something. He has the big beard. He blows on my hand and he wakes me up. When I wake up I say, 'Padre Pio! Padre Pio!' He is trying to say, 'You have to look after yourself.' I am a diabetic. I was in a coma one day last year and he woke me up. I saw him as a shadow. When I woke up from my dream I could see the shadow go out of the room. I ended up in the hospital critically ill. He told my sister last year, 'Tell your sister to look after herself or else she is going to die.' He has helped me many times.

I go to him all the time. All of us Italians worship Padre Pio more than anything in the world. In every village there is his statue. When I go to Italy I go to his shrine. I go three times a year to see him in San Giovanni Rotondo. I save money for him. We make a collection, my family here. We make a collection of all the staff here every night. I bought half of the organ in San Giovanni. I bought two chairs for the church, for devotion to him. I get pieces of cloth that are put into the glove that used to cover the wounds in his hand. I get them from the people that are in charge of the church. They give them to me and they bless them. I come back and I give them to all the people. I have given away 4,000 to 5,000 relics to people that are critically ill. They ask me for Padre Pio relics all the time.

I give them to people who travel by plane, who have a long journey, who go to America or Australia. I give them to people with cancer tumours. I give them to people in trouble with drink or a bad marriage. People come to me and say, 'Pray for my father, he is dying.' People come back to me and say, 'My mother is well, she was saved; she didn't die.' They say, 'My child is well.' It's incredible. I love him because he saved my son, he saved my daughter and he saved me. I love him for what he is. I can't explain how lucky I am to have him in my house. I tell you, Padre Pio is alive and anything I want he has given to me.

NIAMH, COUNTY KERRY, RECOVERED FROM HODGKIN'S DISEASE.

In late 1998 I wasn't feeling well. I was feeling tired and I was going from doctor to doctor. I had put on what we thought was puppy fat around my face. I was 16 and I didn't take that much notice. But Mum and Dad and everyone around me saw it. It was Mum who met our GP on the street and said, 'Look, I'm really worried about Niamh.' The GP said, 'Send her for an X-ray.'

It was only on sending me for an X-ray that they saw I had a tumour in my chest. It was quite large. It all happened very fast after that. Mum pulled me out of school to have the X-ray. I went to the doctor around late afternoon and by nine o'clock the next morning I was in hospital in Dublin. By then it was January 1999. Soon after, I was diagnosed with Hodgkin's disease.

The gravity of it didn't really register with me. All I wanted to know was would I get better. Once the doctor said I would, that was fine by me. I tend to be a very trusting person. I don't know if they were just telling me to help me get through but

I tend to believe people. What hurt me the most was Mum and Dad. I knew I needed strength for what would be a tough journey ahead but I especially knew I needed strength for my parents and family.

The next day they did a biopsy to determine what type of cancer it was. They put me under general anaesthetic. Then, instead of taking the tubes out, they gave me the first round of chemotherapy. They kept me under sedation for about ten days and I was asleep for that time. I was in the intensive-care unit.

Padre Pio entered my life during those ten days. Somebody brought a Padre Pio glove to me but I don't remember it. From then on, Mum was gearing to getting me to San Giovanni and Lourdes. That was what we were working towards from the moment I woke up. That was her promise. It was also my promise that when I was well enough we would go.

After that I had to go through the whole chemotherapy process. It was a tough road. It was all about getting me well and praying. There were times when I wondered would it ever come to an end and would I ever get there. There were times when I felt low after losing my hair and things like that. For a girl, that was a huge thing. It was hard seeing my family upset. At times like that I did need strength and I did need Padre Pio to be there. I do feel that he was there for me.

I didn't finish treatment until the ninth of the ninth, ninety-nine. I had two weeks of radiotherapy at the very end. The treatment lasted right into September. We went to San Giovanni the following summer. Mum and my aunt and I went together. I was looking forward to going and by the time I got there I was really excited. We went down to see his tomb. We were in San Giovanni for a few days.

Our group leader wore a cross around his neck, which is a first-class relic of Padre Pio. He had never taken it off but he gave it to me to wear for a full day. I clutched it all day, it was something so special. There was Mass arranged at Padre Pio's tomb and I got to do the reading. It was an honour. It was absolutely beautiful, it was so serene. I also went to the little gift shops and I brought home a book of Padre Pio's letters to all his spiritual daughters. I used to read one every now and again and I felt I was really one of his daughters.

I am eight years clear of cancer now. I have devotion to an awful lot of saints but Padre Pio definitely has a special place. I had faith and I believed, and I knew he was going to be there to help me through it. Underneath my pillow at night I have medals that touched his tomb and touched all the relics all along the way. I have a miraculous medal and one of Padre Pio around my neck. He helped me to get over the fear and I wasn't afraid. I had my faith and that was all I needed.

MARY, COUNTY WATERFORD, TELLS OF A NEIGHBOUR'S MIRACULOUS RECOVERY FOLLOWING A FALL FROM A HORSE.

A young girl, 12 years of age, was riding a pony up by her home when the pony shied and she was thrown off. She was on the road for about three-quarters of an hour. Nobody thought anything of it, that she was missing or anything. Her mother eventually went looking for her and found her unconscious on the road. She was taken to a nearby hospital where she was kept for about three or four weeks. She had major injuries to her spine and her back. There was no hope for her.

She regained consciousness after about a fortnight but she was semi-paralysed, they thought she'd never walk again and they didn't think she'd live. A group of local people then decided they should give some assistance. So we collected money to help with medical expenses. We gave it to her mother, who was very depressed and very down, with no hope. Unfortunately, the girl then developed pneumonia. The prognosis was very grim.

Before that I had dealings with Donald Enright, who brings

one of Padre Pio's mitts to people in need of help. We got him down with his mitt. The girl had pneumonia the day he arrived and was critical. They were all sitting in the house, crying. Things were bleak. He prayed over her with his mitt. The mother told us that from the day he arrived she turned around. There was a dramatic recovery from that day on. He never had to return to her again.

She spent six months in rehabilitation after that, but that was just to help her physical recovery. She then went on to do her secondary school and she went to college. She now lives a perfectly normal life. I find it extraordinary what happened. I had gone to see the girl a good few times when she was sick and there was no hope, they had no more to do for her. I believe it was all down to Padre Pio and his intercession. I definitely believe it was his presence.

RITA, WHO ONCE LIVED IN COUNTY CORK BUT WHO NOW LIVES IN LONDON, DESCRIBES HER SON JOHN'S RECOVERY FROM DEPRESSION AND HIS SUBSEQUENT ORDINATION AS A PRIEST.

My son wasn't very well. He was in his early 20s. I was in Kinsale and he was in London at the time. He had just finished a university degree in Belgium. We couldn't diagnose what it was. He lost every bit of energy and he was very frail. He lost a lot of weight. He didn't want to communicate with anyone. He wasn't going out. In fact, he seemed to be completely unable to communicate and wasn't talking very much. His father had died some years previously, at the age of 43, and I think it was a delayed reaction to his death.

He came over to stay with me and I really didn't know what to do. I think he was in a deep depression. He was going around like a zombie. He had huge anxiety. I remember on one occasion having a very old school-friend in and I thought he would join us. He couldn't, he left straight away. It wasn't like he had a broken leg, it was much more worrying.

One Saturday I had to go further out into West Cork. I was so fearful of leaving him on his own. I remember my concern as I left. It was the first time I had left him alone. Someone had suggested in Kinsale that they knew this man who had a Padre Pio glove. He came that day when I was gone. John wasn't very religious at the time. However, the man prayed with him. He said to this friend of mine that he had rarely seen someone so frail.

When I came back and drove up to the house, I could see my son standing by the window. I thought, 'My gosh!' He was usually slumped in a chair. I could see a marked change. He said, 'The man was very kind. I certainly feel a bit better.' After that he seemed to gain in strength. He said he felt stronger after the visit. He then got better slowly. He developed more energy. He eventually went back to London and was staying with my daughter although it wouldn't have been convenient for him to stay with her for long.

Then, a strange thing happened. He was out for a walk and he met someone who asked him where the local church was. John indicated where it was. The following day there was a meeting of a lot of young Christian people up in Hyde Park. He came face to face again with this person. John didn't recognise him but the young man recognised John. The young man invited him for a cup of coffee. John said, 'Yes.' He mentioned that he was looking for somewhere to live. He ended up moving in with this group of people who were instrumental in him deepening his faith. He got a job which he wasn't very enamoured of. Eventually he became a priest. He was ordained in June 2006, approximately 20 years since he felt unwell. He had a long journey.

An interesting thing was that my husband had died from a brain tumour. The neurologist who had looked after him said there was very little likelihood that any of my children would have a similar occurrence. He said, 'If you have any worries do contact me.' I wrote to him when John felt unwell. He arranged a scan which showed a slight shadow. Later on, when John went back for another scan after the visit to Kinsale there was no sign of it.

I also remember that when I was carrying John I was diagnosed with a non-malignant tumour in my leg. They didn't do scans in those days. They said I would have to have the operation straight away in case it was cancer. I remember saying to the surgeon, 'Could this mean I would lose the baby?' He said, 'Yes, there is every possibility.' The pain was so bad that I was tempted to go ahead and have the operation. But I decided to wait.

I remember having to rest up in bed. One day my husband brought me in *Journal of a Soul* by Pope John XXIII. By the time I had it finished, all had settled down and I went on with the pregnancy. I had been warned that he might be very badly affected because there were so many X-rays. But when he was born he was absolutely perfect. As a result, I called my baby John after Pope John XXIII. He was a blessed child from the very beginning.

I think the visit was significant. John is a very good priest. He has no anxiety at all. There is no evidence of what was there at that time. I think this was an answer to prayer. I certainly believe that the man with the glove was sent that day as a result of prayer. What happened to John was probably a miracle and it came from God through the intercession of Padre Pio. Also, a lot of my friends in Kinsale at the time were praying for John because they were so concerned for him. I'm a strong believer that God heals. I think it was all the prayers that did it.

PERFUMES AND VISIONS

AN INTENSE AND MYSTERIOUS AROMA OF ROSES, violets, lilies and carnations has been reported by Padre Pio devotees, including those from Ireland, ever since the first pioneers made their way to San Giovanni Rotondo. Sometimes referred to as the 'odour of sanctity' or 'aroma of paradise', the fragrance is often likened to the smell from a garden of roses or, occasionally, incense and tobacco. Appearing mysteriously and at the most unforeseen times, the perfume is frequently taken to indicate that prayers have been heard, graces have been granted or that more prayers are called for.

The celestial smell of perfume has been associated with Padre Pio since shortly after the first visible appearance of his stigmata in 1918. Initially, this divine fragrance emanated from the blood seeping from his wounds. It could also be discerned from his clothes or bloodstained bandages and mittens. Soon, however, aromas were being detected in lands and continents far away. Sometimes, the scent followed prayer to the friar or accompanied the granting of a blessing. At other times, the fragrance reminded recipients of forgotten promises or unfulfilled intentions.

Although similar perfumes have been associated with

other saints, including St Thérèse of Lisieux and St Martin de Porres, no rational explanation for their existence has ever been found. They occur in the absence of man-made scents, flower beds or floral arrays, frequently in open spaces or in the heart of winter and sometimes with remarkable intensity and duration. Scientific and medical assessments, particularly in the case of Padre Pio, have failed to establish their provenance.

Accompanying the following Irish accounts of these odours are testimonies concerning visions of Padre Pio. Like his perfume, Padre Pio's ability to be in two places at the same time or, since his death, appear in the strangest of locations has become part of his legend. Stories of his presence high in the sky, with outstretched arms, defying Allied bomber pilots who were about to attack San Giovanni during the Second World War, are the material of history. Recent stories are more prosaic although no less astonishing.

Sometimes dressed in his simple brown robes, other times swathed in heavenly attire, he has reputedly appeared to those who are sick or in need in many parts of the globe including Ireland. As the following stories reveal, his appearances are reported at times of need, often at the height of a medical crisis, comforting and consoling, bringing relief from pain and suffering while effecting miraculous cures.

SAMMY REVINS, COUNTY CORK, HAD A WIFE WHO DIED OF CANCER.

I never knew Padre Pio until sickness came along. My wife Mena had cancer. Unfortunately, it was lung cancer. She had only a year or a year and a half to live. One of the lads at work was telling me that his daughter was sick and was in bed for many years. She was about 17 or 18 and he told me that they went to a man who was involved with Padre Pio's movement. I got his address and I went up to Cork and we met him. From that day on we got involved with Padre Pio.

I read an awful lot of the books on Padre Pio and we used to pray every night to him.

Then, one Sunday morning I got the smell of the roses. I thought it was beautiful. I got such a fright. I was lighting the fire, I went out for coal and the fragrance was out of this world. I looked around, there wasn't a sinner about. It was before first Mass. It was about April or May. I had no garden, I had no flowers. I went up to herself and I said it to her. She said, 'Yes, I got it before.'

About a fortnight before she died we were in bed together and she said to me, 'Will I play the tape of Padre Pio?' I put it on and some time in the morning she woke me and she said, 'Do you smell that, Sammy?' I said, 'I do, it's like cigarettes, like cigar smell.' I got up. They were all in bed, all snoring away. He came again, that was his presence again with us. You see, Padre Pio will come to people in this way to let them see that he is there, that he is with you.

There was another night, coming near the end, and she tried to wake me. I used to be awake quite a lot at night. This night she couldn't wake me. When she did wake me I was in a ball of sweat. She said to me, 'He was here.' I said, 'Who?' She said, 'Padre Pio.' She said, 'I couldn't wake you, I am frozen but you are wringing with sweat.' That was her privilege and he came to her. 'It's either one thing or the other,' she said, 'either I'm not going to live very long more or I'm going to get better.' I asked her what happened. She said, 'He came into the room. His two big eyes were lighting up. He came over and I was getting afraid. I turned towards you, but he said, "Don't be afraid." He put his hand on my shoulder and that was it. He went then.'

One thing she asked me to do was that I promise that I would go to San Giovanni for her. I said I would and I did. I will never forget what it was like when I got there. When I arrived at the church that evening, it was like as if someone pulled a screen across me and put everything out of my mind. The peace and the happiness and the contentment that was there was out of this world. The time I went there was during the vigil on the night that he died. I remember during the Consecration I said, 'Will this be the end or will you still be with me?' John O'Keeffe was standing alongside of me and the next minute there was a smell of violets, it was beautiful. I said to John, 'Do you get that?' 'No, I can't,' said John. Padre Pio is always there, he'll always help us and he always has.

NANCY SURLIS, COUNTY SLIGO, EXPERIENCED THE SMELL OF ROSES AND TOBACCO.

We had Margaret McDonagh down from Galway with the Padre Pio glove. She came here to a hall in town, to an open meeting with hundreds of people. She was showing a film on Padre Pio and then, afterwards, she let everyone bless themselves with the glove. I went with my sister-in-law. At that time I didn't know much about Padre Pio. I didn't know about the perfume or anything like that.

Like other people, I went up to bless myself with the glove. My cousin was very ill in America at the time, she was dying from cancer and I blessed myself for her. When I did, I got this perfume. It wasn't like any perfume you can buy. It was like the sweet smell you would get off a fresh rose in a garden when roses are in bloom. It was very intense. It lasted only while I had the mitten in my hand, for about a minute or two. It couldn't have been an ordinary perfume, I didn't wear any and nobody around me did either.

I then handed the glove over to my sister-in-law. I can still remember to this day that I handed it over with my left hand and I said to her, 'Isn't there a lovely smell off that glove?' She said, 'There's no smell off it at all.' I put my hand up to my face and I could still smell it, it was still on my hand. Nobody else got it either. I was surprised. My sister-in-law told me about Padre Pio's perfume and she suggested we go up and ask

Margaret about it. Margaret said, 'It does happen.' I told her about my cousin and she said, 'She will probably be healed.' And so she was. I found out afterwards that my cousin in America improved almost immediately. On that very evening she started to get better and she was eventually healed.

The strange thing about it was that she died four years to the date afterwards. She hadn't been well with a kidney infection. I was at a retreat that afternoon and I had no mitten near me. In the church I got a smell of tobacco. It was like pipe tobacco, not cigarettes. It was strong and it lasted a while. It came and went in waves. I looked around the church to see if there was anybody there that had been smoking but there wasn't. I had heard that tobacco smell wasn't good. I had asked in San Giovanni and they said it could mean it wouldn't be good news. I was suddenly afraid that something might have happened to one of my sons. When I came home that evening they had the news for me that my cousin had died of kidney failure. She had got an infection that they couldn't control.

Some years afterwards, my own health wasn't that good. I had a miscarriage and there were serious problems. I was sick for a good while. Eventually, I was able to go back into church although I was feeling weak. After Mass I had been thinking about what I could offer God in thanksgiving for my health when, suddenly, I got the smell of roses again. I was just getting up out of my seat to go across the church to start the Stations of the Cross. The smell was coming up from the ground and was hitting me in the face. It was really strong.

I had to keep going because people had known I was sick and I thought that if I sat down again they'd think I was really ill. I stood at the first Station of the Cross. I knew it was Padre Pio. I said, 'Padre Pio, what do you want from me?' The thought immediately came into my head that I should give Rosary beads to Father Peyton. He was in India at that time and I asked would the Rosaries be any good to him. I was told, 'Yes, he is crying out for them.' So that's what I did, I gave money for Rosary beads. Although it's over 25 years since I first encountered Padre Pio's perfume, nobody can take it from me. What happened is totally real.

CHRIS HAYES, COUNTY TIPPERARY, RECALLS HOW THE SMELL OF PERFUME SIGNALLED HER SON'S RECOVERY FROM A NEAR-FATAL ACCIDENT.

When my son was 12 he was involved in an accident. He had just started secondary school. He used to cycle into school every day. Turning in the gate, a car came around the bend and threw him in the air. He was badly injured. He was in the intensive-care unit in the local hospital and he was so bad that initially he couldn't be moved to Cork. However, the following day he was in such bad shape that they had to move him.

When we went down to Cork the story was far from good. He had swelling of the brain. He had bleeding and a fracture on the left side of the skull. That's what the CAT scan revealed. He was put on a life-support machine. We were given that information in Cork on the Thursday. We were told not to come down on the Friday because that was the day they would be doing tests on him. So we came down on the Saturday instead.

As it happened, within one hour of his accident I had received four Padre Pio relics, little prayer leaflets with third-class relics. I held on to one of them day and night until it fell asunder. I put one of the relics under his pillow down in Cork and I rubbed his head with that relic. I also found out later that on the Saturday morning a man had come in with the glove of Padre Pio. I knew none of this when I was there on the Saturday. We just went in and stayed around all day. They then told us to go home and that there was absolutely no point in staying around.

When we were coming out of Cork the car filled with perfume. I am allergic to perfumes of all kinds. I don't use perfumes and I don't use soap. I can't because I'm allergic to both of them. If I sit beside someone in church who has perfume on them, I have to move away. It was so bad that I checked everywhere. I checked the radiators, everything, to see what the problem was or where it was coming from. I didn't say it initially to my husband, who was with me. But I did mention it to him later and he couldn't get any smell.

At the time I knew nothing about Padre Pio's life. I knew nothing about this phenomenon of perfume. I didn't even know there was such a thing as the stigmata. I just wasn't interested, I suppose. Yet the smell was overwhelming. It was a beautiful, soft, warm smell of perfume. It was an unusual smell but I would regard it as perfume. I couldn't tell you what kind of perfume it was. If anything, it was the smell of flowers. The truth was I couldn't figure out what, in the name of God, this was about or what was happening.

We came eventually to a factory where the grass had been newly cut. We got out so that we could smell the grass, to prove that I and my husband had a sense of smell. Before I got out of the car my back was roasting, so much so that I had to sit out from the seat. I couldn't get out of the car. It was the very same as if somebody was standing behind me with their arms around me, holding me fast. It was the most incredible sense of being minded. It was vivid and real. I could not get out of the car. I really began to get frightened. I thought that maybe the grief and upset of my son's accident was sending me off my head. Anyway, my husband got me out and I was fine.

When I got back into the car the smell was there again. I also had this heat in my legs and back and this sense of being minded and held fast with the strength of arms around me. We got out at a church later on and the exact same thing happened.

I could hardly get out of the car and I struggled to get into the church. When we came back out, we headed for home. Later on in the trip there was a chicken farm. The smell of it invaded the car. When that smell went, the perfume was still there. Then, the perfume just vanished as if it had never been there in the first place. At no stage could my husband smell it.

We came back home and I was very upset, very bothered. I didn't know what this was about. I rang a local curate who had been very kind and good to us, who had christened my son and who had come into the hospital to visit him. I told him what had happened. He was very excited. He knew all about Padre Pio. He explained the phenomenon of the perfume to me. He told me where I could get a book on Padre Pio. I went and I got it. The first thing I did was flick to the pages covering the perfume.

When we went to Cork the following day, I brought the book with me and I was reading it. My son was on a life-support machine for all of that week. He was then taken off it and was unconscious for a further week. On one of the days before regaining consciousness, he suffered two seizures. The doctor took me aside and told me that he would be paralysed down the left side because there was no movement from his left hand or foot. He said he would suffer seizures for the rest of his life. This is what we were facing. We were devastated.

The priest said to trust in Padre Pio and keep praying. We did. I also read loads of other books to find out what this was all about. My son eventually regained consciousness. He wasn't well immediately but he became well very quickly. He had physiotherapy. He went back to school. He did his Leaving Cert. He is now married with a family. The only legacy he has is a scar on his chin where the windscreen cut it. That was 21 years ago. And that's how Padre Pio changed our lives.

A WOMAN, WHO WISHES TO REMAIN ANONYMOUS,
DESCRIBES THE SCENT OF ROSES AT A FUNERAL HELD IN THE
DEPTHS OF WINTER.

I attended the funeral of a young man called Hugh Wright
who died of cancer, who had been ill for two years. He had
great devotion to Padre Pio. On the day of the funeral we
were going through the graveyard when I began to notice this
beautiful perfume of fresh roses. You don't get it today; it was
like the roses when we were young.

I looked around to see where they were growing but there
wasn't anything there other than grass. It was also the beginning
of January and rather cold. I said to myself, 'They must be
on the coffin.' But they weren't. I said, 'Somebody must have
poured the scent of roses because this is overpowering.' I went
along with that.

It stayed for a long part of the walk. Then, a man I knew
asked me had I anything belonging to Padre Pio on me. He
had given us Rosary beads the previous night belonging to
Padre Pio, to say the Rosary. I said I had given them back.
He said, 'That's not what I mean, have you anything on you
now?' I said, 'No.' He then asked me if I smelled the perfume
of the roses. I said, 'Yes.' I asked another person there if she
smelled the roses too. She said, 'Yes.' Another person later
said he had smelled them as well.

I couldn't have imagined it because I wasn't even thinking
about it. There was no thought of any such thing in my mind.
I wasn't even thinking along those lines. It was real, almost
as if there were beautiful fresh roses there. It was like as if
you had come out on a spring morning and the roses were in
bloom. It was as if you went into a garden of roses early in
the morning.

I hadn't thought about it until the man asked me if I had
something belonging to Padre Pio on me. I knew they were
roses but I didn't associate them with Padre Pio. I'm not a
tremendous devotee of his although I would have prayed to

him sometimes. But I will always remember it, it sticks in my memory. There must have been something happening there.

KATHLEEN CONNOLLY, COUNTY MONAGHAN, ALSO GOT THE SCENT OF ROSES.

One time I was in hospital with arthritis. This woman had lovely beads of Padre Pio's. She had cancer and we were very close together. I said to her, 'They are lovely beads.' She said, 'Would you like them? I'll give them to you.' She gave them to me. I appreciated them and I asked her, 'What can I give you for those beads?' She said, 'Send me a Mass bouquet and that will do for the beads.'

Then I went to Knock one Sunday when everyone got together for Padre Pio. By then, the woman who gave me the beads was dead. I went into the chapel and I said to myself, 'The first prayer I'm going to say on the beads is for Angela.' I did a decade for her. When I was doing the decade the smell of flowers came flowing around me. The smell was the loveliest scent of roses you ever got. It filled all around. The scent was flowing all about me. It was lovely and I thought, 'There is something in this.'

I then went to the Basilica for the blessing and the people beside me in the seats couldn't believe where the lovely smell of roses was coming from. I was in the middle of the room and I turned around and said it was coming from the Rosary beads I had. I told them what had happened to me in the chapel. It's a smell that never leaves you. It came back up on me again and there's still a bit of scent in the beads to this day.

I still have those Rosary beads. The beads are very special to me. I also have a Padre Pio statue and pictures. Sometimes I go and put my hand on his head and I rub it on my own. I also do a decade of the Rosary every night for all the saints. But Padre Pio comes first.

ELLEN C., CORK, RECOUNTS HER FAMILY'S EXPERIENCES WITH PADRE PIO'S PERFUME.

My little boy had problems with his tummy when he was very young. He was in and out of hospital. I took him to a lecture on Padre Pio in the Savoy in town. They were showing these slides. I said to my son, 'When the man brings the relic around, you put your two hands up to it.' He did that and so did I. When we were coming out the door he said, 'Mum, you know the thing the man brought around? My hands clung to that and there was a lovely smell from it.' I didn't know about the aroma from Padre Pio at that time.

Another time, I was in San Giovanni and I brought home three Rosary beads for the children. They were on the floor in the sitting-room. They were arguing about who would get which colour. I handed them out. My son got a white Padre Pio Rosary beads and there was a smell of perfume off it for two weeks afterwards. That's gospel. I could smell it too. There was no smell off the girls' Rosaries. My husband brought it down to the priest in the church and the priest said, 'Yes, there is a smell of perfume.' It was a beautiful smell.

I then went to San Giovanni one time with my sister. When we got there my sister was very ill with a sore throat. When I looked out it was pouring rain. My sister said, 'I can't get out of bed, you go up to the tomb.' So I spent some time at Padre Pio's tomb saying the Rosary. I was sitting down. The same people were there all the time. No one came or went. I was at the fourth mystery of the Rosary and I thought I got a smell. I said I wouldn't take any notice of it but it went up my nose. If somebody had come along I would have said, 'Somebody has perfume, take no notice of it.' But nobody had moved the whole time I was saying the Rosary.

I was saying, 'Is that your perfume, Padre Pio?' I kept saying, 'Will I tell my sister? Will I tell her when I go down? Will I tell her in the morning?' I burst into the room when I went down. I said, 'I have to tell you something, I'm sure I got

Padre Pio's perfume praying above at the tomb and I never got this before.' She said, 'You did, because while you were above I was praying to Padre Pio for you that something good would happen.'

BETTY MORAN, COUNTY KERRY, SMELLED HIS PERFUME TOO.
We got this beautiful perfume when we were in his cell being shown around. It was most unusual. It was a lovely sweet aroma. Some perfume you'd be sick after, it would be too strong. But this wasn't, it was mellow. I like perfume and it was most unusual. It remained on you and you smelled it for a long time. It lingered on even after we left. Even if you thought about it, you'd get it. There were no flowers in the room or anything. There were a good number of us there, about 30 of us, but only a few of us got it. You felt that whatever you were praying for, your prayers were being heard. That was his way of letting you know he was listening.

KAY HARRINGTON, CORK, GOT THE SCENT OF ROSES DURING HER RECOVERY FROM HODGKIN'S DISEASE.
Back in 1973 I was diagnosed with Hodgkin's disease, which is cancer of the lymphatic system. Both of my parents were ill at the time so the shock was severe. I wanted to be there for my parents' sake. I also knew that the shock of me having cancer would kill them, so I decided to tell them instead that I was anaemic and had to have treatment. To the best of my knowledge they never discovered the truth.

From 1973 to 1975 I went through chemotherapy and radium therapy and I had my spleen taken out. I had a nervous breakdown when I found out what I had and I also suffered the death of my dear mother in the middle of it all. However, some wonderful things also happened. For example, I met my future husband just before I entered hospital. A friend also gave me a book on the miracles of Padre Pio. Having read it, I put my trust in him.

I was in and out of hospital at the time because I didn't

get all the treatment at once. During one of the slack periods I heard that Donald Enright was taking a pilgrimage to San Giovanni Rotondo and I decided to go. There were 30 people on that trip in July 1975, including my future husband Pat and my aunt and uncle.

As part of the trip, we visited the little church in Pietrelcina where Padre Pio first prayed and we saw the tree he prayed under. It was a very small church and our group only barely fitted in. While we were waiting for Mass to begin I got this overwhelming perfume of roses. I turned to my aunt, who was next to me, and she said she was getting it too.

Later that day I was taken down to Padre Pio's tomb. Although everyone can go down nowadays, it was a great privilege at the time. I was with an American lady by the name of Vera Calandra, whose daughter had a bladder that had re-grown, which was a medical miracle. She prayed with me and I prayed and cried.

I went back to the hotel and crossed the room to tell my aunt about my experiences. She said that as I came towards her there was a wonderful smell of roses, although on this occasion I didn't get it. Later that night, the woman I shared my room with said that as I came in the door she got this beautiful perfume of roses although, once more, I didn't get it.

As we were leaving San Giovanni, a strange thing happened. When we were about 20 miles down the mountain, a thought came to me to look for my passport. It was missing. I had to tell Donald Enright, which was very disturbing for me as I thought I had upset everyone else. Donald said he would ring the monastery to see if I had left it in the shop. Father Joseph Pius answered the phone and said he would check. He rang back to say he had found it and would drive down with it. At this stage I was hysterical at the thought that I had upset so many people.

When Father Joseph Pius arrived, he came into the bus and said, 'Here's your passport.' He also said, 'And Padre Pio is giving you a passport to a new life.' How true it was. In thanksgiving, I have run a trip to Knock and to Holy Cross every year since 1980 although I had to discontinue Knock as I couldn't get enough people that late in the year. Thanks to Padre Pio and all the good doctors whom the Lord directed, here I am 30 years later. I am thankful to the Lord for my sickness because I think it made me a better person.

KAY THORNTON, COUNTY DUBLIN, EXPERIENCED A SOMEWHAT DIFFERENT AROMA OF PADRE PIO.
My sister Emer had a very bad heart and she got a bad heart attack. She was quite young at the time. Things were bad. The doctor went into the neighbour and said, 'Emer is not going to last.' We sent for the priest, who anointed her. As soon as he unscrewed the jar for the oils, there was a very strong perfume of incense. It went right through the room. I thought it was from the oils but I asked the priest was there any kind of perfume from the oils. 'Not at all,' he said. She made a fantastic recovery. I don't know how many times she came out to San Giovanni after that.

NOREEN HANDLEY, COUNTY DUBLIN, DESCRIBES THE SCENT FROM A PADRE PIO RELIC.
We stay in the hotel in San Giovanni that Padre Pio requested to be built. Once, as we went in, I noticed this priest walking around. I said, 'There's something unusual about that man.' I asked our tour guide, 'Who is that person?' She said, 'That's the man that Padre Pio asked to build this hotel.' I said, 'Introduce me to him as quick as you can.'

He had no English. He was a lovely, cuddly, gorgeous man. He put his hand into his pocket and he took out a mitten. Through an interpreter he was telling my daughter and I and a few other women around, 'Padre Pio gave me this mitten.'

The story goes that this particular priest was an altar boy for Padre Pio all his life. At one time, when he was about 12 years of age, he had TB and Padre Pio put his hand on his chest and he was instantly cured.

He went on to serve as an altar boy and he wanted to be a priest. He asked Padre Pio for advice. He said, 'You're not going to be a Capuchin. I want you to found an Order for the relief of suffering, the same name as on the hospital.' The man did, and he has this Order running. One time, he was looking out the window of Padre Pio's cell. His cell has a long window beside it, where Padre Pio used to wave his handkerchief to crowds of people each night at around five o'clock or half past five. He'd say goodnight and they'd be singing hymns. But, looking out that window, Padre Pio said to this priest, 'Do you see that patch of land over there? You're to build a hotel there for the pilgrims.' That's the hotel we stay in.

Anyway, this man, when we met him, put his hand in and took out this card about two inches in length and folded over. When he opened it there was a piece of bandage about an inch long. He told me that Padre Pio had given it to him. It was from his heart wound. He opened it out and the smell of roses was unbelievable. It was a beautiful, sweet smell of roses. It's different to any other rose you'd ever smell. I was so moved I was in tears.

BETTY HENNESSY, COUNTY CORK, ATTESTS TO A STRANGE VISION WITNESSED AT SAN GIOVANNI IN THE LATE 1980s.
I wasn't meant to go to San Giovanni. A friend of mine told me one day that she was going to Rome and San Giovanni. I didn't mind going to Rome but I had no interest in going to San Giovanni. I didn't even like the look of Padre Pio, he scared me. However, I got the last ticket for the flight, it was a cancellation and I went. It was a six-hour or seven-hour journey from Rome to San Giovanni. On the way, people stood up and told all these different stories. They were incredible.

We arrived on 25 May, his birthday. I remember seeing this big bronze statue of him outside the little church. He had flowers placed in his hands. Women were standing around crying. We tried to get Mass but it had finished. The next morning we heard Mass next to the crypt. I remember an Italian woman, dressed in black, pointing at a brick which had an image of his face on it. It left an impression on me.

That morning two women in my group went to where Padre Pio had heard Confessions. It was his Confessional, with a little footstool. His chair was there, with the wood worn away from where he rested his arms. There were bars protecting the room so that people wouldn't take bits of souvenirs away with them. One of the women said to me, 'Can you see him?' I said, 'Who?' She said, 'Padre Pio.' I said, 'No.'

The next morning I was drawn to the same place. I was drawn up there to see what those women had seen the day before. Looking through the bars, I couldn't believe it. I first saw the face of Our Lady. It then changed into Padre Pio. And it then changed into the Passion of Christ. The image was in the middle of the room, about the size of a picture. It had a cloud around it, it was ghostly. It didn't last very long. I was riveted to the spot.

I was frightened. I couldn't believe it. I looked around to see if anybody else was there but there wasn't. I was on my own. Later, I told the spiritual director who was with us. He had never seen this before. I also told the women that night and they believed me. Another man I told said he had seen Our Lady and Padre Pio but never the Passion of Christ. I couldn't get over it.

I came back a different person. I am religious enough but I had no time for him before. Even his image in pictures frightened me. Since then I have said his novena every morning. I've always said since that we are a lucky family. Somehow, I think I was meant to go to San Giovanni. It has changed my life.

AMANDA COYNE, COUNTY CORK, TELLS OF A VISIT FROM PADRE PIO DURING A CRITICAL ILLNESS.

I was 31 years of age and I was expecting twins. I had a little boy already, called Joseph, who was nearly two. I had problems in my pregnancy. I was admitted to hospital weeks before the twins were born. I had very high blood pressure. I wasn't well. Through a lot of mishaps I had an emergency section on 20 May 1992 and the blood clotted. The clots travelled to my heart, lungs and kidneys and shut them down. It was horrendous what happened. Only one in 200,000 would survive it.

The following day would have been my son's second birthday. On his birthday my mum brought him up to visit me and I had gone into a coma. I wasn't aware at all of what was happening around me. They roused me from this very heavy sleep and they called the doctor. I remember the doctor saying, 'Cardiac arrest, room 107' or something like that. I was wheeled to intensive care and I was in a coma for approximately two weeks. What happened in that time was that I had a heart attack and kidney failure and I was in this deep, deep sleep.

My husband brought up a man called John O'Keeffe, who had a first-class relic of Padre Pio. He had some of his beard in a cross. He came to visit me and, apparently, he gave me this ring that he had with a picture of Padre Pio on it. I took it and it would only fit on my thumb because I was so swollen. He had really big hands; he was a fisherman. The ring would only go on the tip of my thumb. I don't remember any of this but they told me later. They only told me because when I came out of this coma I said to Tony, my husband, 'You'll think I'm cracked but I can see Padre Pio's face on my thumbnail.' He went on to tell me then how John O'Keeffe had been up and the story of the ring.

When I came out of the coma I was pining in bed every day for my two-year-old who was at home with my mum, living 30 miles away. The girls, Julie and Edel, were away in neonatal all the time and they were brought over a couple of times a day. I'd wake in the morning and I'd have tears running down my face. I was crying in my sleep. I cried myself to sleep, cried all night and I woke crying in the morning because I missed Joe so much.

I was in bed one day in the hospital. I was lying there praying. I was conscious and I was on dialysis. I was blasting heaven for not allowing me home to my child. I was begging to get home. Suddenly, Padre Pio appeared to me at the end of the bed. It only lasted about ten or twelve seconds. He was in a brown habit with a cream belt. He had his two hands up in an open, prayerful position. He wasn't smiling or laughing. He was very serene and had a nice, pleasant face and he just nodded once or twice.

That night my husband came in to visit me, as he did every night. I had a catheter inserted because my kidneys had failed. As he came in he always looked at this bag and it was empty all the time. Every night he'd look at the bag and look up at me and I knew by his face that the bag was empty. I never knew because I was in the bed and couldn't see what was in the bag. That night Tony came up and he looked at the bag and he just screamed because it was full. My kidneys had started back.

The two doctors that looked after me linked arms with each other and did a jig around the end of my bed. They could not account for it. My kidneys came back and started working. I was passing urine. I came home from hospital after about ten weeks and I was on dialysis four times a day for about a year. It was tough going with three babies. But my kidneys got better and better and better and I eventually came off dialysis.

Today I have high blood pressure and high cholesterol as a result of the pregnancy. We went from two salaries and one baby to one salary and three babies. However, I had been saying to Padre Pio in my prayers, 'I don't care if I never work again, I'm quite happy to go home to rear my children.' That was my prayer and it was answered. That's exactly what I got and I have three wonderful children now.

John O'Keeffe is a saint to me. And Padre Pio has never, ever let me down. I have passed on his prayer to so many people. Sometimes, even in a bus queue or in a queue in a shop I'll get talking to someone and his name will come up. The whole thing put everything in life into perspective. I now have about 40 per cent kidney function and 80 per cent heart function. I'm fine. I envy people their energy. I wouldn't be able to play golf for long or as often as my friends, but who cares!

NOREEN HANDLEY, COUNTY DUBLIN, SAW PADRE PIO AT HER SON'S WEDDING.

In 1999 my youngest son was getting married. At the time of the wedding he actually had pneumonia. The morning of the wedding we didn't think he was going to get through it. He couldn't even stand. He was so weak he should have been in hospital.

He was brought down to the cathedral earlier. He was as white as a sheet, he looked terrible. He said to me, 'Mam, if you see me bending over, catch me.' I was sitting in the front seat. In this cathedral there were six steps up from the altar rails and then it was flat up to the altar. It was a very big place.

As I went into the cathedral I had a funny sensation of the presence of my parents, who are dead. I said, 'Oh, Mam and Dad, just get him through the day.' Then I thought, 'Mam was into Padre Pio.' So I started saying, 'Oh, Padre Pio, please get him through the day.'

Just before the girl he was marrying was coming down the aisle my son and my husband, who happened to be the best man, came down the six steps. As the bride was coming in with her father I looked up at the altar and Padre Pio was standing behind my son. I looked quickly to see if there was any reaction from anybody and nobody had reacted. When I looked back again he was gone.

The first thing that came through my head was, 'Is my son going to die?' I then said, 'I don't think I was imagining that, I did see it.' But with nobody reacting I said, 'Maybe I imagined it.' I was saying things to myself. My son seemed to be fine getting married and I took photographs of the couple holding hands walking up the steps.

Later on in the day, my son was dancing away. He was dancing with me to a tune he had picked called 'My Son'. The words are very moving. I said to him, 'You seemed fine.' He said to me, 'Mam, something very spiritual happened in that church today.' I said, 'What happened?' He said, 'When the bride and her father were walking down the aisle I saw an aura around her.' Actually, on the video of the wedding you can hear him saying to her, 'You're glowing, you're glowing.' He told me that when he held her hand to go up the steps a tingling sensation went from his bride to him and he felt OK.

I never told him what happened to me and I never told my husband. But about three weeks later we were getting the photographs developed and there was Padre Pio's face in the photograph! I knew I wasn't imagining this. I brought it down to the photographer and I got it developed much larger in all sorts of finishes. It was there, very visible. I said to myself, 'Why have I got this? There's a reason for this.'

I still kept looking at it but I never said it to my husband. But one day, on the phone, one of my other sons said, 'Did you hear that my brother saw an aura?' It was a blue and white aura, which seemingly is a healing sign. I let it slip that I had seen something too. So I told him and I told him about the photograph. Then, my husband asked me for it and he saw it straight away.

I had it for months and I was wondering about it. One day I rang the Capuchins. I didn't say what I had. I just said, 'I want to speak to a priest, I have something I'd like to show him.' This priest told me to contact another Capuchin. I rang him on a Monday. I didn't tell him what I had but I said, 'I have something I'd like to show you.' I said nothing about Padre Pio. He made an appointment for the Tuesday a week and a day later, at twenty past seven.

I went up and was brought into a room. This priest came in and he had a big pile of photographs of Padre Pio from the time he was young to the time he was old. I hadn't mentioned Padre Pio. I thought, 'This is funny, how did he know I wanted to talk about him?' I showed him the photograph and asked his opinion. He looked at it and looked at me. He said, 'What happened?' I told him. His words to me at that time were, 'I can't categorically say it's Padre but the longitude is there.' I said, 'What do you mean the longitude?' He said, 'The Padre had a long forehead.' I have since got to know this man very well and he has said to me, 'Oh, yes, that was Padre but I couldn't say it at the time.'

He asked me, 'Have you been to San Giovanni?' I said, 'No.' He said, 'If you go, bring a copy of this with you.' That was in 1999 and this was the start of the pattern. From then on, every time I woke up this thing was going through my head that I was to go to San Giovanni. I was very busy at the time, running a business. I couldn't go anywhere until the end of October. There was one pilgrimage going out to San Giovanni on 27 October that year. In July I booked to go on it.

In the beginning of September one of my grandchildren, who was three and a half at the time, was suddenly diagnosed with a malignant brain tumour. He was living in England at the time. I flew off to England the following morning. The news wasn't just bad, it was drastic. He went in on the Monday and had the operation on the Wednesday. He had a tumour the size of a golf ball embedded in his brain.

When the results came back from the test, they said it was

the worst form of cancer and he had three months to live. They said, 'He will not reach chemo.' Before I left Ireland I had rung the Padre Pio office in Dublin and Eileen Maguire had told me there was a place up near Charing Cross station where they had a Padre Pio mitten. I rang and told them about this child. At the time, the child was in a coma after ten hours of surgery. I cried on the phone with the woman and she said, 'We've never done this before but you can have the mitten overnight.'

We then had the mitten on his head all night. When I left back the mitten, as I was handing it back the aroma of roses practically knocked me down. There was also something like a brown hue beside me. I turned around and there was nothing there. But I could see a vision of brown beside me. I said to the woman, 'Are you pressing a button or something?' She said, 'What's wrong?' I said, 'The smell of roses is unbelievable.' She didn't get it but she said, 'Oh, that's Padre, if you get that it's to say he has heard your prayer.'

The child had another surgery about a week later to remove a portion of his skull at the back. He was home after about ten days. He didn't speak for nearly two weeks. They then did radiotherapy to his brain and spine. They said it was only to prolong his life. They said if he survived he would have stunted growth and all this type of thing. He went on, anyway, to have chemo. He nearly died on two occasions. But that child is a ten-year-old now and he was three and a half when it happened. He's completely healthy. He's the only one under six who has survived this particular disease in England.

They said a Mass for him on 2 November at the tomb of Padre Pio in San Giovanni, which was the day he was starting the radiotherapy. I hadn't told them he was starting the radiotherapy that day. Father Michael Duggan, who was saying the Mass, said, 'I'm going to dedicate the Mass to this little child.' A little later, when I was in San Giovanni, I begged and begged Padre Pio and I said, 'Look, if you help this child and let him live, if you leave him here to do some good I'll help you.' I hadn't a clue what I was going to do.

When I came back around December I said to my husband, 'I've made a promise but I don't know what to do.' It started to go through my head that I was to start a prayer group. So I started the Malahide, County Dublin, Padre Pio group in January. It has blossomed since then. I have a choir there. I have a priest with a mitten and everything else. The crowds we've had have been chock-a-block. The prayer group is absolutely full every first Friday of the month. That was the start of it.

EILEEN REA, CORK, ALSO HAD A VISIT FROM PADRE PIO.
I used to read about Padre Pio when I was a little child. I used to go into school with these cuttings from the papers and I would be crying because this priest was bleeding. I lost contact in my teenage years. Then, 30 years ago, when my last child was born I was very ill and so was he. They didn't expect him to live. I was in my bed that night and this stranger came in with a leaflet of Padre Pio. There was a priest in with me at the time and he said, 'Put your faith in Padre Pio and everything will be fine.'

As I was going to sleep I thought there was a very warm glow around me as I was talking to Padre Pio. I said, 'Please save my baby, go upstairs, mind my baby, put your arms around him and if he'll make it I'll make it.' The following morning the nurse came in and she said, 'Mrs Rea, hurry up, get better fast, your baby made a remarkable recovery during the night. We now expect him to live.' After that I had a great devotion to him.

Then, in 1981, I was very sick after what was the twelfth operation on my stomach. That year there was the unveiling of the monument to Padre Pio down in Rochestown. I wanted to go down but I couldn't. My husband went with my two little lads. I had five children altogether and the two youngest went with him. When he came back in I said to him, 'I still don't feel very well. I'm going up to bed.' I felt as if there was something growing inside of me, and I was only after having an operation three months previously. Nothing would convince me but that I had cancer.

That night Padre Pio appeared at the end of my bed after I had said my Rosary and said my prayers. He was dressed in pure, pure white, trimmed with gold. There was a most magnificent pink surrounding him that I never saw before or since. He had the most beautiful look on his face. There were no stigmata on his hands but of course the stigmata had disappeared when he died. His two hands were held out and he spoke to me. He said, 'Please do not be afraid, you do not have cancer. You will undergo one more operation this week and in no time you will be home to your family.' He did the sign of the cross and he left. I said, 'If this is true, I'll visit your tomb.'

I picked up the phone the following morning, rang my doctor and he came down. I said, 'I have to have another operation.' 'Who is filling your head?' he said. I was afraid to tell him it was Padre Pio. He examined my tummy and he said, 'Yes, you have to see a surgeon this afternoon.' I saw a surgeon at two o'clock. I was in hospital before five o'clock. I had to be prepared for an operation and the operation was done on the Friday. You will recall that Padre Pio's words were, 'You will undergo one more operation this week.'

What they removed that time was a very large benign tumour, which was like an octopus. That's what I felt growing in my tummy. There were legs coming out of it. It was spreading. It weighed about six pounds. It took me six weeks before I arrived home to my family because I got a clot in my lung. I used to talk to the doctors and nurses, saying, 'I'm going to be fine, I'm going to be fine,' because I had Padre Pio's assurance.

I told the truth to one nurse and she said to me, 'No wonder you are so brave.'

I have no doubt Padre Pio was the person who looked after me. He looks after me daily. I'm like a bad neighbour; I'm always asking him for favours for people. If I forget to thank him I'm upset that night. So I continued my devotion after that, which was the biggest experience I had. As a result, I have gone out to visit his tomb 20 times. He keeps calling me back. And I've never had a problem again.

JOHN CUNNINGHAM, COUNTY MAYO, SAW PADRE PIO WHILE IN HOSPITAL FOR CANCER SURGERY.

In July 2004 I wasn't feeling the best. My stomach wasn't feeling right. I was afraid to go to the doctor. I was in Dublin one weekend, up in the zoo with the grandchildren, and I wasn't feeling right at all. I came back and went into work on the Monday morning and I got really sick. I was trying to vomit and not vomiting. I had to drive 40 miles home. I was home around six o'clock and I went to see the local doctor. He said, 'I'll give you tablets and we'll see how you are in the morning.'

I had a very bad night. I was then rushed into Mayo General Hospital thinking that I might be only a week or a fortnight in it. The minute I went in they told me that I wasn't the best and I'd have to have surgery. They thought that I had a tumour in my lower bowel. They didn't know whether it was malignant or not. The hospital were brilliant and I was well looked after.

I was due to have my surgery on a Monday in the middle of July. On the Wednesday night before I had the surgery, at about nine o'clock, I was lying on the bed and the family were there. I suddenly thought I heard footsteps. I was looking around me. I thought I could hear a person walking on black terrazzo. The people around me started to turn into what I thought at the time were Franciscans, even my wife and family and the people in the beds around me. I thought I was dying. The sweat was pouring out of me.

All of a sudden, this man with a beard passed me. I had heard him walking towards me. I could see Padre Pio. He had an eye that was kind of looking at you. No matter which angle you looked at him from, he was coming at you. He just passed the bed, out the door and disappeared into thin air. I said, 'What's happening to me? Am I seeing things?' I could see a tabernacle as well. I was lying in the bed and the sweat was literally pouring off me. The trance lasted for about a minute or a minute and a half. Then I came out of it and this woman, Madeleine Forkan, was standing at the foot of the bed and she had Padre Pio's glove in her hand.

She came over to the bed. I had known her for quite a while. I could see tears in her eyes. She blessed me with the glove and she said the usual prayer. I said, 'If I ever get out of here I will go to San Giovanni, I will go to prove what I saw in the vision was true.' So I had my treatment and I had my surgery. When I was going in for surgery on the Monday I got another slight vision of him. I was in surgery for about three and a half to four hours. They took out a malignant tumour from the small intestine. It was about the size of a golf ball.

I haven't looked back since. When I went into hospital I was fifteen stone. After a full month lying on my side I went down by three stone and two pounds. At the present time I weigh fourteen and a half stone and I'm not overweight. I haven't had a pain or ache since I came out of the hospital. I'm feeling great. It was very successful.

I am big into Lourdes but I'm not over-religious and I was never big into Padre Pio. But all of a sudden I said, 'This guy has something to offer.' I really took what happened to heart. So we went to San Giovanni a year and a half later. We went down from Rome by coach. I walked into the old church in San Giovanni and, believe it or believe it not, there was the black marble going down the aisle to the altar and there was a bronze statue of Padre Pio over the tabernacle in the old church. It was the same Padre Pio I saw in the hospital. Everything that I saw in the vision in the hospital was the exact same as what I saw when I went into the church in San Giovanni.

Ever since then I have believed in him. I am convinced that Padre Pio was a big help in my recovery. We have his picture in the house and I have read books on him. There is one thing certain, as far as I'm concerned, which is that he's there and he's genuine and there's no doubt about it. But he will never let you forget. I go to bed every night thanking him. If I forget about it, I feel him nudge me. I know he's not looking for thanks, don't get me wrong. But I feel in my heart that, apart from the good medical help I got in Mayo and Galway, there was another being there and that being was Padre Pio.

DONALD ENRIGHT, COUNTY CORK, WITNESSED THE MOST EXTRAORDINARY VISION OF PADRE PIO AT MASS IN SAN GIOVANNI.

During 1975 I had great reservations about the time I was devoting to Padre Pio, to the sick and suffering and to giving lectures. I was married, with a wife and four young children. I was travelling all over Ireland and letting my family on their own a lot of the time. I was thinking of giving up the work. I prayed and prayed. On previous occasions I was getting his perfume at lectures or in the car. Now I was getting none.

I travelled out to San Giovanni for the anniversary of his death on 23 September 1976. While there, for two or three days I prayed continuously and without any sign whatsoever. I entered Mass for the anniversary of his death at midnight. Gemma di Giorgi, who was born blind but who had perfect sight as a result of a visit to Padre Pio, recited the Rosary. At one o'clock, approximately 33 priests and bishops came onto the altar.

Shortly after the Mass commenced one of my group turned to me and said, 'Do you see Padre Pio on the altar?' I said, 'Yes.' We both saw him dressed in a brown habit, standing up on the altar. He looked probably around the late 60s. He was facing down towards us, looking the same as in life. Within a short time, a crown of thorns appeared on his head and a look of excruciating agony was on his face. The man in my group saw this also.

It then became the face of Jesus, with a crown of thorns on his head. Then, within another short time, my companion turned to me and said, 'Who is the beautiful young girl on the altar?' I said, 'It's Our Lady.' She was dressed in white with beautiful auburn hair and a crown of gold on her head. At the back of the church, behind the altar, hundreds of stars appeared to be twinkling. I wanted to die and go to Our Lady.

Jesus Christ then appeared on his cross at Calvary. My companion saw Jesus but he didn't see the two thieves. Jesus appeared to be in the last hour before death. There were beams of light shining down towards me from his wounds. The bad thief was hanging on the cross with his head down, in a dark haze. A beam of light from Jesus' hands was shining on the good thief and he was looking up at Jesus. That then disappeared completely.

When it was Communion time, Padre Pio appeared in the golden vestments of a priest. He put his hand in the ciborium. His eyes were glowing orbs of light. He took out the host and walked down through the church to me with the host in his hand. My companion said, 'Do you see Padre Pio coming down with the host in his hand?' I was throbbing with emotion. My colleague held his arm around me, supporting me.

I cried out to Padre Pio, 'Please do not put the host on my tongue.' As far as I was aware, others could see what was happening and I didn't want them to. I didn't want to come back to Ireland and have thousands of people coming to my home. I closed my lips and put my head down. After a short time I looked up and Padre Pio was walking back up through the church with no host in his hand. At the end of Mass, as the priests went to leave the altar, Padre Pio again appeared dressed in a brown habit and he walked behind them off the altar.

From that time on I realised that I would keep my promise and dedicate my spare time to the sick and suffering. I realised that what happened was a re-enactment of what happened every day at Padre Pio's Mass. I spoke to my companion many times about it since. He has written two accounts of it and they concur with mine. He was shocked but thrilled and delighted afterwards to have seen what he saw. I have told about 20 people about it. No one else saw it happen. The one thing I realise is that I was unworthy of receiving this wonderful grace.

TOM MULLIGAN, COUNTY KERRY, RECOVERED FROM WEIL'S DISEASE WITH THE HELP OF AN APPEARANCE FROM PADRE PIO.

Back in 1992, when I was 62, I got Weil's disease, which is spread by rats. I was very bad with it. I went from sixteen stone to twelve stone in four weeks. I couldn't walk, couldn't do anything. I couldn't keep anything down. I was throwing up all the time. I was hooked up to a circulating pump in hospital because they were trying to clean out my blood. They were putting fluid through me. I couldn't move because of the pipes. I was like a dog tied to a post. I was seven weeks in hospital, five weeks in intensive care. The doctors said I was finished.

I had no interest in Padre Pio before that. It was my wife had the interest and knew somebody. She got in touch with a man who came down and he gave me a few holy medals. She got me a small picture, about three inches by two inches or something like that. It had a medal and a prayer with it. I prayed to him. I was on my own in a room so I was lonely and I prayed a lot to him or talked to him. I asked him if he could help me and be my friend.

One night, after about two weeks in the hospital, I woke up from my sleep and I saw him looking down at me from the wall. He looked like he looks in pictures. I was half sleeping and woke up. There was a holy picture and something else on the wall. I saw him where the holy picture was. Instead of it being the figure in the holy picture, it was Padre Pio. To me it was him. He was looking at me through the side of his eye, it was a sideways picture. It was only the top of his head and his shoulders. He had darkish hair, a beard and he looked around 55 or 60. He was looking down at me in the bed. He said nothing at all.

I felt good and got better after that. It took a year to get fully well, it was a slow process. I prayed to Padre Pio most of that time. I believe he had a role to play in my getting well. Something worked, anyway, because I did get better and I wasn't meant to get better. I pray to Padre Pio still, once in a while, and I certainly believe in him.

MARIAN SHEEDY, COUNTY CLARE, ALSO EXPERIENCED PADRE PIO'S PRESENCE.

I go up to the House of Prayer in Achill. There was a time when Mass was said there in the chapel but they don't say it any more. There was a big crowd there and I was sitting down the back. This woman came in with a handicapped girl, around nine. She was really jerking and making noises. She was standing and nobody got up to give her a seat. I went over and said, 'Do you want to take my seat?' Then I went up to the front of the church where I saw a vacant seat.

The priest was saying the Mass. Just before it was over he turned to me and he beckoned and said, 'I want you up here beside me.' I thought he wanted a glass of water or something.

He said, 'I want you to stand here and hold this in your hand and face the congregation.' He handed me a picture but I never looked at it. I just held it. I was embarrassed because I am shy and there were hundreds there that day. He then said, 'I have the glove of Padre Pio. If anybody wants to be blessed, come and queue up.'

I was standing there for over two hours and they came up in the hundreds and he blessed them with the glove. They then kissed the photo. When it was all over I turned to see the photo. Of all the pictures I had ever seen of Padre Pio, I had never seen this one of his face. It was most unusual and most strange. I knew about Padre Pio, his wounds, that he was a friar and that he lived in San Giovanni, but that was it. I didn't pray to him. I prayed to St Anthony and St Francis. However, on this occasion I got to handle and touch his glove and then the priest blessed me.

The following month, when I went there again, I was sitting in the back and looking up at the priest. There was a wall at the side of him where they had the statue of Our Lord and there was a big blank space above that. My eyes were on the wall and I was listening away to the priest. Suddenly, through the wall this image like a photo negative appeared. I was looking at it as it materialised on the wall. I rubbed my eyes and I turned away. It was the side face of Padre Pio that was coming out from the wall. Above him, more faint and not as prominent as Padre Pio, was the face of Jesus with the crown of thorns on him. I could distinguish it and say, 'I know what I'm looking at here.'

After that I came home. I was above in my bedroom some time afterwards when this magnificent smell of roses came all around. I was saying a prayer to him at the time. I didn't class it as roses at first. I thought it was my daughter had invested in a new deodorant. I said, 'Wow, what is that? It's magnificent, what brand is that?' I came out of the room, smelled around the bathroom, smelled the landing and went in around the corner to her bedroom. The smell wasn't there but it was heavy inside in my bedroom. A couple of days after that I started putting two and two together and said, 'I wonder was that the smell of roses you get when Padre Pio is near you?'

After that incident I decided to find out all about Padre Pio. I said, 'I will go to the library.' By the time I got there I had forgotten that I was to check him out. Before I knew where I was, I found myself over in the religion section. I don't remember rooting through the shelves but I took up volume one and volume two of a book of Padre Pio's. This is going back a good few years before computers, when they put a stamp on the books. I took them home and they were his letters to his spiritual director.

I started reading and I remember being overcome up in the bedroom. I cried my eyes out especially over what he had suffered. I read of the Devil and how he could transform himself into Our Blessed Mother and how the guardian angel with Padre Pio always knew who he was actually dealing with. I was amazed. After some time I gave those two books back. They were small, navy-coloured and hard-covered.

Some time down the road I said, 'I really should have taken notes from them.' So I went up to the library. I looked and saw no sign of the books. I went to the woman and I said, 'Could you check for these books, has somebody taken them out?' I told her about the books. 'Oh, no,' she said, 'we never had those books.' I said, 'You did, I took them out of here and you stamped them. I have read them.' She said, 'When?' I told her. 'Just a second,' she said. She looked again. 'I'm sorry,' she said, 'we never had those books.' I couldn't argue and I came away astounded.

I said, 'I'm definitely going to check this out.' I was in Galway and I went into bookshops. I got them to check branches around the place and they said they never had them.

So where did the two books come out of that I read? A long, long time later I was reading *The Irish Catholic* above in bed. I was flicking through the pages. I suddenly let an almighty roar out of me. I couldn't believe what I was reading. Here was this article about Padre Pio and his letters to his spiritual director. It said, 'They are now going to be translated from Italian into English.' The emphasis was on the *now*. I said, 'What is this? I've already read those two books.' Yet nobody could find them and nobody had any record of them.

I was a Eucharistic minister in our friary. Our guardian came up one night when I was really pondering over all this. He said, 'What's wrong with you?' I said, 'I don't think I'll tell you for the simple reason that you won't believe me.' He looked at me and said, 'Try me.' I said, 'I know you are sceptical about these things but I have had a very strange experience.' I told him the whole story. He said, 'That would be Pio. If he wanted to make himself known to you, he'd find the way.' That's the end of the story and I'm amazed by it.

Why this happened puzzles me. I prayed to St Francis and St Anthony. But I think Padre Pio wanted to make his life known to me. Why? I don't know. I was in a very bad accident and I nearly died. I was given the grace of a deep conversion. A load of things were happening to me. Maybe that was it. I have devotion to him since. I say my prayers to him. He is on my bedroom wall. He's on my dining-room wall. I don't like flying so I mightn't ever get to Italy. But he's now on my list and I always pray to him.

KATHLEEN CONNOLLY, COUNTY MONAGHAN, EXPLAINS HOW THE TURNING-POINT IN HER ILLNESS OCCURRED AFTER AN APPEARANCE FROM PADRE PIO.

I had an operation for a burst appendix a few years ago. I was in hospital for a long time. I was 74 years of age. I was a very sick person. I was near dying. I took a heart attack and I'm lucky to be living. There was no hope. My biggest problem in hospital was that I could not sleep. I was closing and opening my eyes and I was saying to myself, 'If only I could sleep for a half an hour I'd be landed.'

One night I was praying and I said to Padre Pio, 'If only I got a half an hour's sleep I'd be very, very happy.' I always believed in him. I'm not great at praying but I might say one Hail Mary to him. I have a statue of him at home. All the time I was sick, my son left the statue on the kitchen window so that anyone coming in saw it. Anyway, I closed my eyes and when I had them closed there came to me the loveliest picture of Padre Pio. I never saw as nice. What drew my attention was a lovely gold colour around the picture, on the edges. I looked at it and I have never forgotten the words that were written at the bottom of the picture, 'There is hope.'

I got my sleep. The nurses came in later on in the morning. This nurse said to me, 'What happened to you?' I said, 'Nothing happened to me.' She came back again a while after. It was the same story, 'What did happen to you? Something has happened.' Eventually she asked me again and I told her the story; that I couldn't sleep, I closed my eyes and was saying a Hail Mary to Padre Pio when this picture appeared with the words on it, 'There is hope.' She said, 'I was thinking there was something because there's a big, big change in you.' The nurses and the staff were very much amazed by what had happened.

They were in and out all that day asking me the same question and I told them the same story. They had wanted me to stay in hospital over that Christmas but I said, 'No, I have had enough of it and I want to be home for Christmas.' So I got home. The only problem I have been left with is a lightness in my head. So I always pray to Padre Pio and I never miss going to Knock for the Sunday in September. I believe it was his intercession that has left me the way I am today. I know I am a very lucky person. I have a lot to be thankful for.

PRAYER GROUPS, VOLUNTEERS AND PILGRIMS

'NEVER GROW WEARY OF PRAYING,' PADRE PIO once said, reflecting his belief in the power and necessity of prayer. Although it was his lifelong conviction that prayer was essential for redemption, it wasn't until 1947 that he instituted the first formal measures to establish a network of prayer groups in Italy and elsewhere. Initially established in 23 Italian cities, each group met monthly under the direction of a priest and with permission from the local bishop. Praying, among other things, for the Pope, for peace and for their own intentions, the groups were, in Padre Pio's words, 'a tremendous chorus, linking heaven to earth and men to God'.

By the time of his death in 1968 there were 700 prayer groups in 14 countries, with a total membership exceeding 70,000. Ironically, the week of his death saw the arrival of representatives of prayer groups from all over the world to San Giovanni. They came with a double purpose in mind. First, they arrived to commemorate the fiftieth anniversary of Padre Pio's visible stigmata, on 20 September. In addition, they came to participate in a convention of prayer groups which began two days later, on 22 September. Although Padre Pio participated at Mass that week and also waved to, and blessed, the assembled crowds, few of those present anticipated that he would be dead within hours, on the morning of 23 September.

It was through the work of pioneering pilgrim and devotee Mairead Doyle that the first prayer group was established in Ireland. Suggested to her by Padre Pio, its informal beginnings can be traced to the late 1960s and its formal existence dated to 1970 at the Pro-Cathedral in Dublin. Inspired by her enthusiasm, the concept spread rapidly. Soon, prayer groups were being set up in rural areas and other towns and cities throughout Ireland, their numbers eventually reaching well into the hundreds. Although the largest single number is centred in the Dublin region, most areas of the country are represented.

In the late 1970s a central Padre Pio office was established in Dublin, which is formally affiliated to the friary at San Giovanni Rotondo. A similar Northern Ireland office later came into existence. Other developments include an annual national pilgrimage to Knock, first established in 1979 and held on the third weekend in September. A pilgrimage to Holy Cross Abbey, County Tipperary, is also held on the last Sunday in May.

Perhaps the most laudable work of the prayer groups is the carrying of Padre Pio relics to the sick and the dying, the distressed and the traumatised in all corners of Ireland. Criss-crossing the country, volunteers bring mittens and pieces of bloodstained bandages to hospitals and homes or to wherever the need exists. Allied to the many thousands who travel each year on pilgrimage to the tomb of Padre Pio at San Giovanni Rotondo, this Irish network flourishes as part of a worldwide movement currently involving 3,000 prayer groups and over 400,000 members.

MARY BRIODY, COUNTY WESTMEATH, RECALLS THE WORK OF HER AUNT MAIREAD DOYLE IN PROPAGATING DEVOTION TO PADRE PIO IN IRELAND.

Long before the prayer groups, in the early 1960s, Mairead had films of Padre Pio and she used to go around the country with them. We used to sell tickets during the interval. We'd be in the Gresham Hotel or elsewhere. Padre Pio was always on to her about prayer. He said to her to go back to Ireland and set up a prayer group. There was no such thing in Ireland. She had to go to the Archbishop. She was almost afraid of what to do. Her first prayer group was set up in 1970.

Padre Pio gave her two medals; one was of St Michael the Archangel and the other was of Our Lady of Grace. The two prayer groups that she was eventually in charge of, she called them St Michael the Archangel and Our Lady of Grace. She also helped start prayer groups in other places. She promoted him everywhere she went. She had two pilgrimages a year and she'd go to meetings all over the place about prayer groups.

Then she'd go to San Giovanni Rotondo on her own supposedly to look at hotels but really she just wanted to go there. In those days the Italians weren't used to tourism. You'd often arrive and your beds wouldn't be ready. She was great dealing with that sort of thing because she took no prisoners. She would do her utmost to do everything dead right.

She worked very hard. She was a huge organiser and she could delegate. She'd often have a Mass, say, for the tenth anniversary or something like that and, as she was a teacher, she'd have all her students helping. I'd be wondering where she got these lads with ponytails. She'd have Austin Gaffney singing. It was a huge thing and she'd do it all on her own without batting an eyelid.

EILEEN MAGUIRE, DIRECTOR OF THE IRISH OFFICE FOR PADRE PIO IN DUBLIN, WHICH IS AFFILIATED TO THE FRIARY AT SAN GIOVANNI ROTONDO, ON THE SPREAD OF THE PRAYER GROUPS.

The spread of the prayer groups was down to Father Alessio. He stayed with my family. He came in 1968 to study English, having spent six years at the side of Padre Pio. While he was here, Padre Pio died. He went back for the funeral but he got permission to return to Ireland to continue his studies. For that year, 1968 to 1969, he went to the English Language Institute, he studied English and he got his exams.

He went back to Italy to start a magazine, *The Voice of Padre Pio*. He became the English language correspondent in San Giovanni. He had, while he was here, gathered addresses. He started writing to people he knew in Ireland and they began to correspond with him. In 1972 he returned to Ireland and this time he wrote a little card to all of those he knew, announcing that he was coming.

So many people came to see him that I had to put my son on the door letting people in. He got requests to go to this and that parish, and he travelled all over Ireland speaking about Padre Pio. He had the glove that Padre Pio had worn and he took it all over the country. He did a tour as often as he got permission. He loved to come. People loved to listen to stories of Padre Pio.

He had slides at the time, and he had a film. He said Mass, spoke about Padre Pio and blessed people with the mitten. He always did this with the permission of the local parish priest. This is when it spread throughout the country because he travelled north, south, east and west in the 1970s. He told people about the prayer groups and encouraged them to form groups of prayer.

Then, in 1978, he did a six-week tour and he was on *The Late Late Show*. He spoke to Gay Byrne for maybe 20 minutes. During the course of the interview he mentioned about being in Synge Street the following evening where we had a meeting organised. After the show Gay Byrne came over to us and said, 'How many does Synge Street hold?' We said, 'Three hundred.' He said, 'You're in trouble because they are coming from all over Ireland, the phone is hopping.' I said, 'I don't know what we are going to do,' thinking of buses from the country and not being able to accommodate them.

The following morning a man called to my door looking for Father Alessio. He wanted a blessing with the glove. His name was Billy Walsh. He said to me, 'Is he in Synge Street tonight?' I said, 'Yes, but we are in terrible trouble, the phone is ringing constantly, people are coming from the country and we can only take 300.' He said, 'Why don't you transfer to the National Stadium?' I said, 'We couldn't do that at such short notice.' He said, 'Give me half an hour and I'll be back to you.'

It transpired that he was a member of the boxing board. Everything was arranged within two hours. We put a person at Synge Street, which is only down the road from the National Stadium, to redirect everybody. The National Stadium held 5,000. It was full and there was a queue down to Leonard's Corner. Father Alessio did what he usually did; he spoke of Padre Pio, of his six years at his side, of the many things he had seen and of the amazing things that had happened to him while at his side. We were there until nearly twelve o'clock and he blessed everybody.

That was a real help to us. We needed help and we got help. Father Alessio was so enthusiastic and he encouraged people to get together and to pray. He spoke about Padre Pio's enthusiasm for prayer groups and he talked about the intentions of the prayer groups. He encouraged people to join prayer groups. What happened then was that you had somebody who was very enthusiastic in an area. They said, 'We want to start a prayer group, what can we do?' We said,

'You approach your parish priest.' In many cases they got permission, they started small and gradually they multiplied. Some fell by the wayside but the prayer groups spread all over Ireland. The devotion spread as a result of his many visits.

The other thing Father Alessio did was to push to have an area in San Giovanni where English-speaking people could go and meet him and the other friars. It was to be like a welcome area. So he covered-in a small courtyard and thus the English office was born. He never served anything there except Irish tea. We always sent out the Barry's tea to him. Everybody that went there brought some. He was well known for his Irish cup of tea, and the Irish were always welcome in San Giovanni.

MARGARET McDONAGH, COUNTY GALWAY, BRINGS ONE OF PADRE PIO'S GLOVES TO THOSE WHO ARE SICK AND UNWELL.

I got the glove from Father Alessio, who had been Padre Pio's assistant for a good number of years. I had been in San Giovanni in 1974 and he asked me would I be a promoter in the west of Ireland. He saw that my address was in Galway when I subscribed to the magazine. I told him I wouldn't. I felt I didn't know enough about Padre Pio. I never really said yes; I was pushed into it. A little neighbour of ours got cancer. I went up and down to Dublin for the relic for her. I was telling Father Alessio and he sent me an envelope with the glove in it. It started from there, from 1976 when I got the relic.

I have seen hundreds of cures since then. There was one man who had cancer and I was called in. His cancer had shown up on X-rays. Lucky enough, I came as he was going to theatre. He said to me, 'I know now I am cured.' I said, 'Hold it, pray to the man above.' 'Oh, no,' he said, 'Padre Pio is looking after me.' He went into surgery, he was opened and there was no cancer there. I think that story was sent to San Giovanni.

Back in the late 1970s or early 1980s another man was in the hospital with cancer of the throat. He was in the last stages.

I was called to go in. He only had a few days to live. When I went in I spoke to him but he didn't respond at all or even move. I thought he was unconscious. He was there on his own. I made the sign of the cross on his throat and on his head, and I asked Padre Pio to help him. I don't do that except when the person is unconscious. Otherwise, I let them do it themselves.

I usually go in on Tuesday and Friday. The next time I went in he was sitting up in bed. His daughter was beside him. He wrote on a page for his daughter to tell me that I took his sickness and pain with me when I walked out the door. I said, 'But you didn't know I was here at all.' He bowed his head indicating that he did. Thanks be to God, he's still alive some 30 years later.

There was a girl who had a very bad heart condition. She is in her 20s now. She had no hope at all. She was in the Regional Hospital in Galway and I was called in. I put the relic on her. I was in and out to her a good few times. I used to hand the relic to the mother and she would put it all over her. That was a very slow healing. But, thanks be to God, all of a sudden she improved and she is great although there was no hope at all for her.

There are so many of them. There's one young woman who got measles, shingles and leukaemia, she got everything. I often said to her, 'You have nine lives, dear, because I saw you dying so often.' She said, 'I kept my faith in God and in Padre Pio and I knew they wouldn't let me down.' She is great now. Also, there is the story of a child, not so long ago, who went to Dublin for a big heart operation. The doctors were surprised when the child went up because they didn't have to do the big operation they thought they would have to do. Things weren't as serious as they thought.

The problem is that I don't hear half of the stories until years later. For example, an older man came to me with something wrong with his chest. He said, 'Would you please cure me

like you cured my grandson?' I said, 'I didn't cure anyone.'
'Oh, you did,' he said, 'you cured my grandson when he was
only two days old.' They had no hope for the child, there was
something wrong with his heart and they had the coffin ready.
He said, 'You were called in with the relic, you put the relic on
him and after that the child was cured. He is 19 years now.'

It's all a result of prayer and faith. It's often you'd see people
who are lukewarm but it strengthens their faith. Some people
haven't been to Confession or to church in a long time. One
man said, 'What's that?' I said, 'It's a relic.' 'Oh,' he said, 'it's
15 years since I was in church.' 'Well,' I said, 'that doesn't
matter, you can bless yourself.' When I came back again he
said, 'I felt such peace, sit down here and talk to me.' The next
thing, he called the priest and went back to Confession and
Holy Communion. That's the wonderful thing.

I see peace and acceptance. Peace comes over people.
When I come back they often say, 'Margaret, after you left
something came over me, it was so peaceful.' They might have
been petrified about going for an operation. I remember one
woman saying, 'While I was in the theatre it was so peaceful.
If this is heaven I don't mind dying.' One woman even said,
'Thank God I got cancer because it brought me back to God.'
You hear things like that all the time.

GEMMA DILLON RUNS A PRAYER GROUP IN NAVAN, COUNTY
MEATH, WHICH STARTED IN 1980.
Our Padre Pio prayer group in Navan has an average
attendance of 300 people every first Wednesday. I also have a
mitten which was given to me by Father Alessio. The stories
we hear are amazing. For example, Michael, this friend of
ours, came to the door one day in a pretty bad state and said,
'My niece is dying in the local hospital with pneumonia and
viral meningitis and she is only two months old.' He shot off
with the mitten. He takes the mitten around the country for
us a lot of the time.

He got over to the hospital just as she was being moved to Crumlin. They said, 'I'm afraid there's not much hope.' He blessed her with the mitten. Soon after she arrived in Crumlin they said, 'This child is not so ill, what's the problem?' They couldn't see any sign of meningitis. Eventually, the local hospital rang Crumlin to see if she had arrived alive. They were surprised to find that the child had even survived long enough to get to Crumlin. She was discharged about nine days later in perfect health and she is fine since. Michael says that his extended family stormed heaven, through Padre Pio, during the trauma and he has no doubt that Padre Pio was present during his niece's illness.

On another occasion, Brother Alphonsus, from the Capuchins in Church Street in Dublin, came down to our Christmas Mass. He said he would bless everybody after Mass. This lady was to enter hospital the following week for back surgery because she was in such extreme pain. She was due for an epidural the following Monday. Her husband had to help her to come up to the altar where she had to stand and wait. Unfortunately, Brother Alphonsus took a long time going from side to side. She was in agony.

Eventually, Brother Alphonsus came by. She said, 'It's my back.' He said, 'Turn around.' He put the mitten on her back. All she can remember is tears running down her face. When she walked away from the altar the pain was almost gone. By the time she got home it had disappeared. Up to now it still hasn't come back, and that's the first time in years that she is without pain. She didn't even need the procedure she was due to have.

Another time, Michael's wife noticed a black spot on his back. He went to the doctor to have it diagnosed and it was a malignant melanoma. He had extensive surgery to remove the tumour. He then had to have treatment. Afterwards, he had an MRI scan to see if there were any signs of it elsewhere and they discovered a tumour on his brain. They were almost completely certain it was malignant, particularly after just having a malignant tumour removed. A second MRI discovered that it was more extensive than they thought.

He had to have surgery. He had it on a Monday morning. The doctor said that the surgery was very extensive and it would be some time before he'd be well. He was up and running on the Monday evening although badly swollen, bandaged, with drains in his head and in a lot of pain. The following day he was so improved that the doctor said, 'You are so well there must be some other influence at work.' He replied, 'Yes, I've got great faith in Padre Pio.' His devotion to Padre Pio is so intense it's unbelievable. The doctor said, 'Something is working for you, hang on to that.' He came home on the Thursday morning and the tumour turned out to be non-malignant.

CÁIT MURRAY, COUNTY MAYO, HAS TRAVELLED FAR AND WIDE WITH A PADRE PIO BANDAGE.

The relic is about three inches by four inches. Padre Pio wore it around the wounds of his heart. It still has the bloodstains on it. When I got it from Father Alessio, in the early 1980s, it was in a little plastic bag. He gave it to me at San Giovanni. It is just like a piece of cloth stained with his blood. I put it into a leather case and I put plastic over it and I got it sewed over twice so that nobody could interfere with it. I'm always afraid that people are curious but it can't be got at.

I couldn't tell you how many people have had it going back over 20 years. Thousands of people have blessed themselves with it, young and old, babies, grandmothers and grandfathers, people who die, just everybody. People take it to their fathers and mothers. Sometimes I look at it and think of all the people who are gone that blessed themselves with it. I also think of all who have survived. And I think of all who could probably tell you more stories than ever I could tell you.

People bring it with them if they have somebody sick belonging to them. Every day, somebody comes and it is gone some place around here. It has been to Canada a couple of times, New York, all over England. Somebody would say, 'I'm going to Canada, my brother is dying of cancer, could I bring it?' I say to whoever is in charge of it that they are responsible for it.

I will tell you a little story about bringing it to England. As it happened, I was going over to an anniversary. A few days before I was going, this lady called me. I knew her, she used to come here on holidays from England and she used to call in. She lived in Birmingham. She said to me that her friend's son had been in a terrible accident and he was in hospital. She asked, 'Would there be any way you could get the relic over?' I wouldn't send it; somebody would have to bring it.

I asked, 'Where is he?' She said, 'He is down in Stoke-on-Trent, in Staffordshire.' I said, 'That's strange because that's where I'm going tomorrow.' When I got there he was really bad. His liver, and everything, was crushed. His mother used to travel from Birmingham to Stoke-on-Trent every day. I went to the hospital. The family were there. I could see he was very ill. I let them bless themselves with the relic and bless him with it. I then left there and forgot about it. I came home and that summer the woman walked into my house and said, 'I have my son outside in the car.' He had recovered completely.

Another strange thing happened on that trip. I had travelled out from Knock. I was pulled aside and searched. The official said to me, 'Can I look in your bag?' I said, 'You can, feel free.' I gave him my bag. He was opening the little purse and I said, 'Be careful with that because it's a relic of Padre Pio.' He looked at me and said, 'You are joking?' I said, 'I am not, that's why I am carrying it in my bag.' He said, 'Can I bless myself with it? I have always wanted to do this.' I said, 'You can.' He then went on to tell me about his mother-in-law who was very ill in hospital and somebody brought it in to her. And she was OK.

A further story involves a nephew of mine who was very ill. He had a sinus infection and he went into hospital. That evening I got a call from my brother to ask me to come to the hospital. He said that my nephew was very ill and was in intensive care. There was no hope for him. They were draining out his sinus and they thought he had got meningitis. So we all rushed to the hospital, although something kept telling me not to panic and not to get excited.

Having blessed him with the relic, I went down to the church around two o'clock in the morning. I was at the altar, kneeling down, and up on the altar was, 'Be not afraid, for I am always with you.' The next thing, my brother tapped me on the shoulder and he said, 'He's fine.' His mother and I went down to the friary to Mass at seven o'clock in the morning. When we came back he was sitting up, eating his breakfast and out of intensive care.

Another story involves a friend of mine whose grandchild was small at the time. She was only six months. The other granny had the child and she was minding her for her daughter. She was getting the dinner. She put the grandchild in the buggy at the door. Next thing, she looked out and the buggy had collapsed. The child had gone forward and she was smothering.

She ran to the neighbour and rang the doctor. The baby was brought to hospital. The granny went up with the relic and there was no response, she was just lying there as if she was in a coma. They were all around the bed. They were all devastated. I said to the granny, 'Go up again in the morning and bring the relic with you.' She went up in the morning around six o'clock and brought it with her again. She blessed her with it and the little one opened her eyes. Everybody got excited, including the nurses. The doctors were called. They said, 'Do something that she would be familiar with.' Do you remember 'The Birdie Song'? The granny started doing it and the next thing the little one started doing it. She was out that evening.

When she came home, they had a picture of Padre Pio at the top of the stairs and every morning, when her mummy would take her out of her room, she would wave at him. It was as if he was waving at her. We never knew because she was too small. When she would be going to bed the last thing she would do, going up the stairs, was wave at him. She is 15 now. It's an extraordinary story.

To go to somebody's bedside with the bandage can be very touching. I think it's very important to be there when somebody is dying. When someone close is dying, people become very irritable with each other. You can see a lot of tension. I always say, 'Let us bless ourselves and the ill person with this relic.' They have come back and said to me, 'The peace and the graces that flowed around that bed were something else.' That is a very special healing.

Sometimes I come out and I shed a tear by myself in the car. If you go to a young man that is dying, or a young mother, they're going to be wondering, 'Who is going to look after the children? Who will mind my children?' It can be very upsetting. I always say to people, 'You must pray, don't think the relic is going to do it, it's only a symbol.' It helps people and it gives people courage. I always say, 'I am not a healer; you must talk to Padre Pio to ask him to go to Jesus to heal you. It's your faith and my faith that does this.'

I'm not interested in worldly goods or fancy houses or fancy cars. My interest is to be kind to somebody and share my love with somebody. That to me is better than anything else. The bandage certainly is part of that. Every day my first thoughts are for the people who maybe rang the day before saying 'I have cancer' or 'I have just been diagnosed. Will you pray for me?' To me, it's a great privilege to be asked to do that.

LUCY CRANNEY WITH THE BACKGROUND TO THE PADRE PIO PRAYER GROUP SHE FOUNDED IN BELFAST IN 1980.

Back in the 1970s my son Damian got convulsions. I was very worried about them. He was just a child. I was also concerned that the drugs the hospital came up with to treat him would affect his formative years and hold him back when it came to school age. As it happened, Brother Laurence, from the Capuchins in Dublin, had a sister living in Belfast and he would come up to visit from time to time. He came and blessed Damian with Padre Pio's mitt.

I also went off with my mother to San Giovanni to pray for Damian. When I came back through Dublin Airport, my husband Frank was waiting with Damian and our eldest girl. I had been concerned when I was away about how Frank would cope if Damian took any of these convulsions. As it happened, his temperature did go up when we were away because he got a bad throat infection and he was on an antibiotic. He had flushed cheeks when I saw him at the airport. I said to Frank, 'Is Damian sick?' He said, 'While you were away he had a very bad throat infection with a very high temperature, but he hasn't taken any convulsions.'

We had promised the children that we would bring them to Scotland as a treat. Damian's throat infection didn't clear up and we went off to Scotland with our sick child. The first night in Scotland I had to call out a doctor and he said, 'This child's throat has been bad for two weeks. I will change the antibiotic and if there is no change 24 hours later I would recommend you bring him home to Belfast.' All I was thinking that night was, 'Why did Padre Pio do this to me? I went over to San Giovanni to pray for Damian and now he is sick.' I was forgetting that what I had gone over to pray about was that Damian wouldn't have any more convulsions. I wasn't seeing the bigger picture.

Twenty-four hours later, on a Sunday when I came back from church, Damian was kicking ball with Frank on the grass outside. He was as right as rain. The antibiotic had kicked in and the child was great. It soon dawned on me that I had received the grace that I had gone and prayed for in San Giovanni. Damian had become a normal boy, able to take normal infections with high temperatures and no longer getting convulsions. Damian went from strength to strength and eventually was taken off his medication. He did well at school, went on to university and excelled himself academically. He is now in his 30s. There were never any repercussions. All my fears were proved to be unfounded.

Following what happened, Brother Laurence said to me, 'The Troubles are very bad in Belfast, there is a great need for a Padre Pio prayer group. If it's God's will, the priest will give you permission.' We lived on the verge of a troubled area in north Belfast. We had lived there since 1969 when the Troubles began. We got permission eventually. So it started on 1 June 1980 and it has been going since.

We are on the fringe of areas where people suffered a lot as a result of the Troubles. They lost husbands, brothers, sons or other relatives. The trauma that was caused by the Troubles also brought ill health. They had plenty to pray for. I have brought groups to San Giovanni practically every summer and also to the Padre Pio weekend at Knock. I think it's been a great help in the 20 years that were very bad in Belfast. Padre Pio understood about trauma and sorrow because of the type of life he had offered to God. He had suffered a lot. He definitely understood the troubles of people in Belfast.

As time went on, my family needed Padre Pio again because there was sickness with other children and we needed his intercession. Then, some years ago, I was at a wedding in Sligo and I had a brain aneurysm. It happened while I was singing a song at the wedding reception. By coincidence, I had the relic of Padre Pio in my possession, which I had got from Brother Laurence through his fellow Capuchin Father Alessio. It was a piece of bandage from the wounds of Padre Pio given to me for our Padre Pio prayer group. It was only brought to Sligo for an aunt of mine. They had brought the relic into the hotel where I was at the wedding reception to return it to me. That's where I had the aneurysm. It was a strange coincidence.

I had to be rushed to Sligo General Hospital. When they diagnosed what was wrong I was put into an ambulance, along with two paramedics and a doctor, and sent off to the Royal Hospital in Belfast. They warned my sister that I might not make the journey home because the bleed in the brain was so bad. My sister held the relic of Padre Pio on my head on the way back to Belfast. I know it's the reason why I am here today and why I had a successful recovery from the brain aneurysm.

I have Padre Pio to thank for everything. What I initially asked Padre Pio's prayers for, I received. In turn, I set up the Padre Pio prayer group little knowing that in later years I would constantly need his help. Every time I have got his help it's like a message that he doesn't want me to give up the work that we do. I think all the things that happened are linked to Padre Pio.

LONG-TIME DEVOTEE KAY THORNTON, COUNTY DUBLIN, WHO HAS A PADRE PIO GLOVE, DETAILS TWO OF THE CURES SHE HAS WITNESSED.

The very first one was the husband of a cousin of mine. He was in St Luke's and he was dying. He was so bad that we weren't allowed to look at him. He was sent home and he was to die before the next Christmas. My mother said to me, 'Bring me up to him and bring the mitten.' We went up to him and he was blessed with the mitten. We prayed to Padre Pio. In no time at all he was walking down the village. The next thing, he had his job back. People were saying he mustn't have had the illness at all but the doctors were clear about it.

A recent one involves a man and his wife from Dundalk.

He was dying with heart trouble. There was no hope at all for him. He needed a new heart but they couldn't get a new one for him. They came to me. They went home and his wife prayed very hard for him. Very soon afterwards, the phone rang and the hospital said, 'Come on in quick, we have a new heart for you.' Eventually he was up here again, saying thanks to Padre Pio, looking very well with his new heart. People are always coming to my house, everybody knows Teach Pio. And there have been dozens of cures, so many I couldn't count them.

ARTHUR BEALES DESCRIBES HIS WIFE BETTY BEALES, WHO IS WIDELY RESPECTED IN DERRY.

She developed devotion to Padre Pio about 20 to 30 years ago. She used to read magazines about him first. When she started doing pilgrimages to Italy she got stronger in her faith in Padre Pio. She would read books. She got on very well with the priests out there. She met the priests who looked after him and she got special privileges. The priests used to let her sit on the bed where he died and on the chair where he used to sit and read his prayers in the little cell where he lived.

She must have been in San Giovanni ten or fifteen times. They knew she had some sort of cure, some sort of power. She had relics of Padre Pio and then she had the loan of a mitt. She asked for a mitt of her own but they had none left. The priest out there said to her, 'I have something more important than that. I've got a bandage that was around his hands. I can give you a piece of that.' So she had a little bit of it. She used to give it to people to bless themselves with.

She knew in herself that she had some sort of power. People started to come to her and she used to console them. People used to come in with loads of bother on them. She used to sit them down and talk to them. After five or ten minutes they'd go out with the burden taken off their shoulders. She'd pray with them and cure them through Padre Pio.

There were people coming in with sore backs, sore heads or confused and going out as if nothing had happened. It happened all the time. People came in with sore legs, bad chest trouble. There were young boys and old people. Some passed out at times with the pressure. I saw grown-ups sitting alongside people who they brought over to see the wife and they passed out themselves. There were thousands of people. It wasn't just Catholics, it was Protestants as well. I've seen bus-loads come up to our street one time. There were car-loads of people coming to see her from all parts of Ireland.

One story sticks in my mind. It was a Saturday morning and it was a good day, it was. I was standing looking out the window. This Post Office van pulled up outside. A man got out and he came up our footpath. He was struggling to get up. He was in his working clothes and I thought it was a parcel or a letter. I answered the door and he said to me, 'Is Mrs Beales in?' I said, 'Why?' He said, 'Could I see her? For God's sake, could I see her?' He struggled in. I went out of the kitchen, out of the way.

I heard him talking to the wife. About five minutes later I heard the front door closing. I came out then. He was going down the footpath and into his van. I said, 'What was that man about?' She said, 'He had sciatica in both of his legs.' He got in his van and away he went. I met him a month or two after that. I didn't know who he was. He stopped me in the street and he said, 'I was up at your house a couple of months back and I saw your good wife and she cured me of sciatica.'

Eventually, the Bishop got to hear about it and he sent for her. He got it organised for the St Vincent de Paul to look after her, to give her a little room up in the Creggan where we live. People used to come in the little room where she used to sit and she'd help them. I was working at the time. She was there one day of the week and I'd come home and she'd say, 'I saw a terrible lot of people today.' It was only one day a week because the Bishop told her, 'Don't do it too much. What you're doing, Betty, is just like me sitting in the Confessional box. It drains the energy out of you. I know how you must feel. Do it just once a week.'

I had sciatica in my leg but she couldn't help me. She couldn't help immediate family. It was only strangers she could help. Then she took ill in about 2004 and that was the end of it. But she cured hundreds of people. She believed it was Padre Pio helping her. She'd say, 'When I used to put my hands on them, on different parts of the body where they were sick, it was Padre Pio doing it not me.'

EILEEN MAGUIRE, DIRECTOR OF THE IRISH OFFICE FOR PADRE PIO IN DUBLIN, EXPLAINS HOW THE OFFICE BEGAN AND DEVELOPED.

By 1979 it had got to the stage where my family home was being engulfed by work on behalf of the friary. Our landing was full of books, my bedroom was full of books and we had people calling constantly. Every time we sat down to a meal it was interrupted. Our home was losing its privacy completely. It had really become an office for the Padre Pio movement. We had four children and they were all at a stage where they were studying. It had become a huge problem for us.

Father Alessio was in Ireland that year and he noticed this. He felt that if we started an office we could get voluntary help. So we started an office in 1979, in Dufferin Avenue, and we got many volunteers coming in. We became officially affiliated to the friary and were recognised by San Giovanni. We now have a full-time secretary but the rest are voluntary. We have the relics of Padre Pio in the office, not just the glove but some bandages and other things given to us, and authenticated for us, by the friary. We also built an oratory where people come to pray privately and bless themselves with the glove.

We allow a glove to go to hospitals. We could not meet the demand for the glove if we had to go ourselves. We found that we would just be back from a hospital when we'd get another request. So we started a diary and we permit the glove to go with the relative of the patient. People come and collect it and bring it to hospitals during the day and return it before evening. It never goes out overnight. That has worked very well. It has brought many letters of thanks for graces received over the years.

I suppose, essentially, the office is a centre for information and the distribution of literature. It's a recognised charity and a link between the friary and Ireland. We promote the magazine, *The Voice of Padre Pio*, on behalf of the friary. We arrange pilgrimages. We assist those who'd like to travel independently. We provide information on our website. It's also a centre-point for group leaders from all over Ireland who come regularly to collect literature, to speak with us and to get information. But our biggest work in any year is organising and promoting the Padre Pio weekend at Knock, which is held on the third weekend of September. We invite speakers and the choir. This has now become the biggest pilgrimage of the year at Knock. They meet to honour Padre Pio and Our Blessed Lady.

We have also seen a lot of graces. One concerns a woman who came one day to the office with a baby in her arms. The baby was born with no movement in her eyes. There was no sight and the future was very bleak. They had been told that the baby wasn't focusing and wasn't using her eyes at all. She came to the office at approximately three o'clock and I said, 'They are about to start the Rosary upstairs; take the baby up to the oratory and tell the group what's wrong and ask for their prayers.'

She went upstairs with the baby and told her story. She was terribly worried, naturally. The group were very moved and they prayed and prayed for this baby. On that particular day one of the older members of the group said, 'There is movement in the baby's eyes.' We all thought, 'This is wishful thinking.' The woman continued to come in as the weeks went on. The news got better and better. Over the course of a year the baby began to focus. That child is now 11 or 12 and her sight is perfect. She has weaker sight than most of us but she can see just fine. The prognosis at the beginning was that she'd have no sight. It was an answer to prayer.

Another story concerns Audrey who came to San Giovanni with us year after year. Her reason for going was that she was suffering from cancer. She was a nurse and she realised exactly what was wrong with her. She had, over about ten years, come out every year. She had great devotion. She prayed to Padre Pio and was absolutely convinced that he was looking after her and would continue to look after her. She liked, when she was in San Giovanni, to go to Confession. She did this every year. And she regarded Father Alessio as her spiritual director.

Eventually we got word that Audrey was not feeling very well. She had got secondary cancer. As it happened, Father Alessio was in Ireland for a very private ceremony and we hadn't told anybody. He was with us at our home in Dublin and nobody knew he was there. Audrey's sister was home from abroad because Audrey was grievously ill. She told me that Audrey wasn't accepting her fate. She wasn't willing to let go. She wanted to book for San Giovanni and go there.

I put down the phone and I mentioned the story to Father Alessio. He said, 'Let's go.' We went to the hospital and, when we arrived, they were amazed. First of all, nobody knew that Father Alessio was in Ireland. Secondly, nobody was even fully aware that Father Alessio was her spiritual director. When Audrey saw Father Alessio she said, 'Eileen, I'd like some privacy.' I left the room. She went to Confession to Father Alessio, she made her peace with the Lord; she was resigned, happy and completely contented.

As I returned to her room that day she said to me, 'I prayed and prayed because I wanted to get to San Giovanni, I wanted to have my Confession in San Giovanni, I wanted to pray at Padre Pio's tomb. That wasn't possible so Padre Pio brought a little piece of San Giovanni to me.' She was very relaxed, very resigned. Her family were so happy because she had received some sort of consolation from Padre Pio in her final days. She died one week later.

MADELEINE FORKAN TRAVELS THROUGH COUNTY MAYO FOR TWO WEEKS EVERY YEAR WITH A GLOVE BORROWED FROM THE PADRE PIO OFFICE IN DUBLIN.

I get the glove from Eileen Maguire for two weeks. I have it booked well in advance, maybe three or four months, because it is heavily in demand. This is the glove that goes throughout the 26 counties. I travel to Dublin to collect it. I leave here in the morning at twenty-five past seven and I come back down at a quarter to four. I start into it immediately after coming down, travelling throughout Mayo, and I get to meet a few thousand people over the next two weeks.

I go to hospitals and nursing homes, people call here to the house and I bring it to Masses. We have it announced in advance on the local radio, in papers and elsewhere. To do the hospital in Castlebar alone is a seven-hour job. We have six Masses, which are always full. People might not be able to come because they might be very ill. Some people ring up and say, 'Would it be possible for you to call or could somebody call to you to collect the glove?' My husband Tom and I are on the road non-stop. He drives me around. We just have a small bit of food or a mineral. We basically eat nothing for those two weeks.

Usually, when I go into a hospital I start in intensive care because that's where most new patients are. I go in there and I bless them all. They are attached to machines and everything. I bring leaflets of Padre Pio and I leave them with the patients.

About eight or nine years ago a woman in intensive care was critically ill with cancer. I knew her very well. Usually, if a doctor is working on the patient I will not intrude. This time they called me to go over. She was unrecognisable, she was that ill. She was given up totally. I blessed her with the glove and said a few prayers. I left the novena on the locker. She recovered and she is absolutely perfect. She is a miracle. She refers to herself as 'the miracle person'.

On another occasion there was a little boy there who had meningitis and he was very ill. His father was there. I said, 'Do you mind if I bless the child?' He said, 'No, not at all.' I blessed the child. I also said to the father, 'Would you like to be blessed?' He said, 'I would, of course.' Then I left and went off to all the other children and infants that were there. I was told later on that the mother had been downstairs and when she came up she said, 'Was there somebody here?' Apparently, she had got a beautiful smell of roses. Her husband said, 'Oh, yes, there was a woman here who left this leaflet and did a blessing with Padre Pio's glove.' The child improved instantly and by the next morning he had totally recovered.

Another girl had a lot of complications with her gall-bladder and her insides. She rang up and said, 'Can I come to the house?' Over she came, herself and her mother. She had a lot of surgery. She prayed with the glove. She maintains that Padre Pio cured her and made her fine. She now comes every year and she thinks there is absolutely nothing in the world like Padre Pio. She actually says that Padre Pio walks with her, she can feel his shadow.

My sister was also very ill with her chest, with asthma. She was in hospital and she was too ill to be moved from Galway to Dublin. I gave her the glove and I said, 'Put it close to your heart and say a prayer every day.' Her husband, to this day, says that she never complained after that. There are so many miracles. I can think of a young fellow who fell off a motorbike and he was critically ill. He was in a coma and in intensive care. I went to him as well and he recovered.

Another woman came up to me at a Mass where I had the glove. She said to me, 'Would you mind coming out to my husband and blessing him with the glove?' I said, 'Not at all.' The poor man had been sent home from hospital and he was hardly able to talk. He was so ill. They had given up on him. He was not eating. I blessed him with the glove. I said, 'Put your trust in Padre Pio and pray for his intercession.' That was three years ago and the man is great, he is perfect. There are dozens and dozens more stories: people suffering from depression, people with all sorts of problems. And all this happens in the two weeks with the glove.

When it comes to an end I bring the glove back to Dublin. I go back up again on the bus. I feel I have done something for people, because there are people out there suffering night and day and nobody cares. People are so busy, flying here and there. Someone might say, 'I have a pain.' The person they are talking to says, 'I have a pain myself.' And that's the end of it. You must show care for people because it's important. So I feel good, I don't feel tired and it gives me great fulfilment.

EILEEN REA, CORK, ON THE CURE OF A BABY SHE WAS ASKED TO VISIT WITH HER RELIC OF PADRE PIO.

I went to a woman who had given birth to a baby in the hospital in Cork. The grandmother rang me one afternoon and said, 'Please go in to see my grandchild, she's not doing too well and they don't expect her to live.' I said, 'I can't go in at the moment because I have young children myself, but I will go in at seven o'clock.' She said, 'That might be too late.' 'No,' I said, 'it won't be too late because I'll ask Padre Pio to make sure everything is fine until I go in.'

I went in to the baby with this relic of Padre Pio. She was in this special-care unit and there were two doctors with her. I pulled back when I saw the doctors because I didn't want to interfere with the medical side. They said, 'No, come.' As I did I got such a cold shiver right up through me. It was like as if I was taking everything from the baby. The baby just started shaking. I said prayers and then I left. As I was going down the stairs I said, 'I must find out where the baby's mum is.' I did. I went up to the ward to her and I said, 'I've just been with your baby; your baby is going to be fine.' She said, 'What?' And that baby was fine, it was grand. It's six or seven now. It's amazing.

People tell me I have a special communion with Padre Pio. I always say that he's my lifeline to the Lord and Our Lady. Padre Pio only intercedes for us and he's my lifeline because I am not worthy to go to the Lord or Our Lady. My house is like a shrine to him. He is all over the house. I have a big statue to him out in my porch for everyone to see. I love him. Nothing surprises me with St Pio any more.

BRENDAN BYRNE, COUNTY CARLOW, WHO FOUNDED A PRAYER GROUP IN COUNTY WEXFORD, REFLECTS ON HIS DEVOTION TO PADRE PIO.

In the year 2000 I had a factory accident. A heavy weight fell down on my head. It was bad. I bled a fair bit. I was in and out of hospital for that year. I can hardly remember a thing. One of my family was told I would end up disabled. Around a year later things were getting back together. About that time I got back to work. I was driving to work one morning and I got a slight turn. It was a form of seizure. The seizures started getting worse. I was getting six and seven a day. I'd fall down and I'd be shaking. I couldn't drive or do what I wanted to do. I ended up in intensive care, connected to tubes and stuff. I got really depressed in myself. I felt like a big burden on my family.

My family, especially my mother and my wife, had been praying to Padre Pio but I hadn't. The Padre Pio glove then came to my home town, where I grew up. My parents and my wife brought me to it. I was blessed with it. I put my hand on the glove and was blessed and I felt a warm sensation. It's really hard to explain the sensation. I got a feeling of peace. I could feel there was something there. Others said they didn't get it. It was only me. From then, the seizures went from six or seven a day to maybe one a week.

The glove came around again. I was brought to it in 2003, three years on from the accident. I got blessed with it again. At that time I got the scent of roses. A few of the people in the room got it too. It was like when you would walk through a garden and stopped to smell the roses. It was really strong. It lasted intensely for a couple of minutes but it stayed with me for a long time, even for the rest of the day. From then on, I haven't looked back.

Before the accident I was lucky if I went to Mass once a year. I just feel that through Padre Pio and Our Lord things got back into shape. I learned the whole meaning of life and not to waste my time. My family and I got involved in a prayer group in Carlow. We got a glove and we bring it around to people. We hear great stories and reports from people who got what they wanted. I became a Eucharistic minister in my local church. I also set up a prayer group in County Wexford. Each time I go back, it has got bigger. It's a great honour to be able to do something and to give something back in return.

After my son was born we found that he had no swallow. He was depending on the tubes. The doctors weren't sure what was wrong with him. It was only later that he was diagnosed with cerebral palsy. When he was born we were told we were bringing him home to die. We were told that he would just lay there, never smile and never communicate. It would only be a while before he was gone. We named him John Paul Pio.

We prayed and prayed to Padre Pio for some form of help.

We knew we needed feeding-machines to allow him to come home. We were told there was going to be a waiting-list on this equipment. It was coming up to Padre Pio's birthday and I was always told that Padre Pio, instead of getting a present, gives a present on his birthday. We were in the little chapel in the hospital. It had just hit midnight and I was praying and praying that we would get home soon. The very next day we got word that all the equipment was in place and ready. That had to be Padre Pio. The baby is smiling away now and making his own attempts at communication. He's flying.

He goes to a special school. We brought the glove there for the little children and their families. A woman came up to me afterwards and she said, 'My son was getting seizures every day but he was brought to the glove and he hasn't had even one seizure since.' He was having seizures all his life before that. It's typical of the sort of stories you hear back.

My family and I are indebted to Padre Pio for what he has done for us. A day doesn't pass now without my saying a prayer to him. People also come to me and ask me to say a prayer to Padre Pio for a certain person because they know how I got on. They feel that because I got better I'd be a bit closer to him. But we are all really close to him when it comes to praying. And he must be one of the closest saints to God, having had the stigmata.

We even went out to San Giovanni in thanksgiving. It was absolutely fabulous. There is an amazing quietness and peace where the tomb is. I wrote a poem about six months afterwards. The poem, entitled 'Your Love', reads like this:

> I often lay in bed at night
> And ask myself, why me?
> You picked me up when I was down,
> You helped to carry me.

You helped me carry my cross,
It wasn't made of wood.
Through all the pain and suffering
You helped me when you could.

Now I would like to thank you,
My family thank you too.
For St Pio, you brought me home again,
We give our love to you.

I know you are helping others
Just like you helped me,
So that I do not ask the question,
The answer is plain to see.

TOM NEARY ON THE PADRE PIO PRAYER GROUP PILGRIMAGE TO KNOCK EVERY SEPTEMBER AND THE HISTORIC CONNECTION OF KNOCK AIRPORT TO PADRE PIO.

The Padre Pio pilgrimage to Knock started back in 1979, the year of the Papal visit. It was a pilgrimage of all the Padre Pio prayer groups. They wanted to be part of the occasion. It was held before the Pope came to Knock, before his arrival on 30 September. Since then, the pilgrimage has kept to the third Sunday in September all through the years. The day before, they hold a seminar with people invited in to give talks, they include a Mass and they have discussion and debate as well.

When they came in 1979, and for many years after that, the numbers varied very little. We would always estimate it as very large, somewhere in the region of 10,000 to 12,000 people and maybe more than that. Not only would the Basilica be full but also the standing area outside and even beyond that. It has been a huge pilgrimage. They use it to consolidate, to keep people together and to keep the interest in Padre Pio going all the time. It's an event they look forward to during the year. And, of course, Padre Pio had great devotion to Our Lady so Knock is an appropriate place for them to go to.

To mark the twenty-fifth anniversary of the pilgrimage back in September 2004, they presented a portrait of St Pio to Knock. It's a charcoal portrait. It was done by an Italian artist by the name of Antonio Ciccione. On the occasion of the presentation, Eileen Maguire, Director of the Padre Pio office in Dublin and the organiser of the pilgrimage, was there. The painting is still on display today, and they also have a life-size painting of Padre Pio permanently in the Rest and Care Centre in Knock.

Also, at the time Knock Airport opened in 1985, when we had the inaugural flights to Rome, one of the places that was included in the trip was San Giovanni. There were three flights that went out that day. They were the very first flights out of Knock Airport. There were over 400 people on that pilgrimage. We went from Knock into Ciampino Airport in Rome. We took them all down to San Giovanni, where they showed us around Padre Pio's cell and the whole place.

Every year San Giovanni sends representatives to the pilgrimage in Knock. I can remember a few years ago there were at least three or four people from San Giovanni, even a couple of lay people as well to accompany the friars. They have kept that strong link going down through the years. So the connections between Padre Pio and Knock live on and are stronger today than ever.

MONA HANAFIN REVEALS HOW HOLY CROSS ABBEY, COUNTY TIPPERARY, HAS BECOME A CENTRE FOR PADRE PIO DEVOTION WHILE HOSTING A SPECIAL PILGRIMAGE DAY ON THE LAST SUNDAY IN MAY.

I wanted something in memory of Padre Pio. I approached Archbishop Thomas Morris and asked him for permission to do a Way of the Cross in memory of Padre Pio. When the Pope was coming to Ireland I wrote to him. I was in Rome at the time looking for someone to sculpt the Stations. It was Holy Week. I wrote to the Pope and asked him would he accept from the people of Ireland a Way of the Cross. I knew he had a garden and it could go up there. I got word on Good Friday that he would accept it. It was all done in a week. So there I was coming home with two sets of Stations to get made, not one, and we had no money.

We set out to collect the money and we got enough to do the Stations for Holy Cross and to do the Way of the Cross for the Holy Father. We presented it to the Holy Father when he came to Ireland. He blessed the two of them. I went back again to the Archbishop and said, 'Look, there are only two sets of these in the world and the mould is broken. There will never be another set.' So we made a garden out of the car park at Holy Cross 26 years ago. I also set up a Padre Pio prayer group that meets every month in Holy Cross and we average about 600 or 700 people.

I also got a beautiful bust of the Holy Father which is at the entrance and which was blessed by the Pope. About five years ago I, and a group of devotees, brought back a second statue of Padre Pio to put on the ground. The other was near the altar and people that were sick couldn't get up to it. The second is now up in the garden so that people can go over and touch it. We see gatherings of over 10,000 people coming to pray. The Archbishop speaks on that day. There are Confessions, anointing of the sick, the Way of the Cross and the Mass. On occasions, Father Ermelindo has come from San Giovanni to give a homily on his years with Padre Pio. It's really lovely. And it's very prayerful.

KITTY CULLEN, WHO BEGAN A PADRE PIO PRAYER GROUP IN BALLYCULLANE, COUNTY WEXFORD, ASSESSES THE GROUP'S PILGRIMAGES TO KNOCK AND HOLY CROSS.

When we go to Knock the 53-seater bus is always full. The people are so happy to go. Some are people who wouldn't be able to go without the bus. We are located about ten miles from New Ross and we leave about six in the morning. We pick people up in our local village of Ballycullane, then we go on to the next parish which is Clongeen, then Newbawn, then to Ballinaboola, Cushinstown, New Ross and then to Clonroche, Enniscorthy, Bunclody, Carlow and on to Knock. We collect people as far as Bunclody. We go in for breakfast in Athlone.

People would be giving out, 'Oh, God, are we leaving that early?' But they like to arrive early because they have Confessions, they can do the novenas and walk around. We arrive there about half past twelve and the devotions for the blessing and the anointing of the sick start at half past two. We have Mass and then the procession and the Rosary. It's over about half past five and then we head back. We arrive home about twelve o'clock or maybe one o'clock in the morning. It's a wonderful day.

It's mostly older people. You get young married couples too, but you're talking from the 40s to the 70s. They love Knock. You must remember that Our Lady was number one with Padre Pio. I remember being up there once for the all-night vigil in December. I was there with another girl. We were coming across the square in Knock. It was overcast; there was cloud all around the place. Suddenly, there was a break in the cloud over to our left. A ray of light came out of that cloud and it shone right down on the church. Everybody was standing looking at it. It was like a yellow glow of light, it was beautiful. It's a wonderful place.

We also go to Holy Cross for the Padre Pio annual pilgrimage in May. It's nearly the same trip. I pick them up around the place, at home in Ballycullane, in New Ross, then on to Inistioge, Thomastown, Bennettsbridge and we go through Kilkenny. We usually have our breakfast in Thurles. We pick up people as far as Inistioge. It's the very same as Knock with the anointing of the sick, the Confessions, the Rosary and all the rest. It's also wonderful. People love it and they wouldn't miss Holy Cross for anything.

I remember being in Holy Cross one wet day. It absolutely bucketed down. We had plastic bags all along the seats. Every now and again we used to stand up and catch our plastic bags and drain the water off them. The Archbishop said, 'Well, I never talked to so many umbrellas in my life.' That's all he could see. Yet nobody got a cold.

People go year after year. One woman must be in her 80s and she hasn't missed one year since I started 25 years ago. People get a lot out of it. They say to me, 'Oh, God, the day was wonderful.' The following week I get all the letters and the Mass cards saying, 'Thanks very much for such an enjoyable day, I feel so good after it.' They are hardly off the bus at twelve o'clock or half past twelve at night when they are saying, 'Thanks very much, we'll see you next year, put down our names for next year.'

Without a doubt, Padre Pio is doing some good for people. People receive so many graces and blessings. One man up in the north of the county had a niece in Canada and there was no hope for her. There were tumours all over her body and she was sent home from hospital. 'When I heard about it,' he said, 'I lit a candle to Padre Pio and I kept that lighting and I kept saying the prayer. She went back again for tests and there wasn't a tumour left.'

People tell me about all sorts of other things like, 'I was to have an operation but when I went into hospital I didn't need the operation.' My own daughter had cancer. I never even worried. I believed in Padre Pio. I never lost sleep over it. I never worried about it because I put it in the hands of Padre Pio and I asked him to pray for us. God looks after us. I kept the candle lighting all the time. And she is grand.

My own husband died ten years ago from cancer. He had a tumour at the bottom of the spine. A very good specialist in Dublin told me when we went up first, 'Ten and a half years is about the life of him.' He lived for nine and a half years.

But for the last two years he wasn't able to get out of the bed. I nursed him in bed and never let him go to hospital. I had nobody, only myself.

I was up night and day. When he'd go asleep I used to go up to the little side church in Ballycullane at four o'clock in the morning. My mind would be so addled that I wouldn't know what I was going to ask for. I'd go in and I'd be so tired that I'd fall asleep. The parish priest used to come in and call me. I'd come out and my head would be so clear, my mind would be so clear and I wouldn't have said a prayer.

Sometimes, when I'm under stress I often feel I'd want to be like Padre Pio – in two places at the one time. I think it's what you put your faith in. I put my faith in Padre Pio and God and the Blessed Virgin. I believe in Padre Pio and I pray to him all the time. I put my faith in them all and they are all good to me.

I have a prayer that means so much to me. It was given to me more than 30 years ago by an old man who is dead years. I never lost the prayer and I always said it. He said, 'If you keep saying that, it will do as much for you as it has done for me.' It goes as follows:

> Padre Pio, up on high,
> You were once a little boy.
> At that time you did not know
> God would one day love you so.
>
> When my troubles are so great
> I will knock on heaven's gate.
> There you will wait for me,
> So gracious in your sanctity.
>
> Dear Padre Pio, help me find
> A way through life both good and kind.
>
> Amen.

HUBERT Mc HUGH, COUNTY LEITRIM, ON HIS TOUR THROUGH LEITRIM, ROSCOMMON AND DONEGAL WITH FATHER ERMELINDO, FELLOW FRIAR OF PADRE PIO AND HEAD OF THE ENGLISH OFFICE AT SAN GIOVANNI, WHO CAME TO IRELAND IN 2006.

My wife Christina and I used to bring down the mitten every year from Dublin and do a two-week tour through Northern Ireland, Donegal, Sligo, Leitrim and Roscommon. Then, in May 2006, out of the blue one evening I had a call from Eileen Maguire from the Padre Pio office in Dublin. She said to me, 'Would you take Father Ermelindo for a week?' I said, 'Who is Father Ermelindo?' She said, 'This is the friar who spent the last three years with Padre Pio before he died.' She said she would like it if we could arrange three separate venues and keep them apart. I said, 'Where is he going to stay?' She said, 'If at all possible, it would be nice if he could stay with you.' We said, 'We'll give it a try.'

We were apprehensive about it. This guy was coming that we didn't know. We knew he might not have a lot of English. But we went ahead and made the arrangements. We arranged a Mass in Strokestown. We arranged another one in the Franciscan friary in Rossnowlagh. We also picked Manorhamilton as quite a big venue in north Leitrim. We then took off to Dublin and met Eileen at the Lucan Spa Hotel, so that I wouldn't have to go through the city. At the time, I had all sorts of apprehension about picking up this friar and what he might be like.

We picked him up on the Monday. He was a lovely guy. The first thing that struck me was his baggage. He lifted this small little bag and that was all his belongings, everything he had. His bag was about the size of a lady's large handbag. I thought, 'Look at all we carry around with us when we are travelling!' Our first call was to see somebody in Mullingar. We started then on our trip, doing a lot of local people who were sick, going to nursing homes, to people who were very ill with cancer and all that.

We then headed to Strokestown on the Tuesday evening, our very first night. More than 700 people turned up at the church. We got to the church at ten past seven and we left at ten past eleven. He said the Mass with other priests and he blessed everybody. What amazed me about Strokestown was the large amount of young people. People came from everywhere, Galway, Mayo, Sligo and Leitrim. It was absolutely unbelievable the devotion to him.

The stamina he had was amazing. He was over 70. He was a very small guy. We had a chair for him to sit on after Mass when he blessed the people. He couldn't sit down because he'd be too small, so he stood up all night until he finished every last person. We then drove back that night. He wanted nothing only the simplest of things; a little bit of breakfast, a poor robin's portion. He liked one glass of wine. Everything was simple with him. He talked about Padre Pio. He told us many stories. He would always say, 'Padre Pio was a very simple monk who went about his business in a very simple way. He prayed all the time, he heard Confessions for hours and he blessed people and prayed with people all the time.' It was fantastic to talk to him.

On the Wednesday morning he did a radio interview and that night we did Manorhamilton privately for people. Then we headed to Rossnowlagh in Donegal. The friary there was full to capacity at twenty past seven for the eight o'clock Mass. It was the same story; he was there until half past eleven that night. He said the Mass and spoke about Padre Pio for maybe 30 minutes. People travelled from all parts of Northern Ireland to Donegal for the Mass, up from Letterkenny as well.

On the Thursday, in the house here, people were free to come and meet him if they were ill. An awful lot of people came. We saw the saddest of cases, mostly cancer, also multiple sclerosis. One guy came all the way from Tuam.

One woman came with this lady in a very sad state. Her little boy of 17 had been killed about two months previously. He was working on a building site, they were unloading a lorry and something rolled off and hit him. He got up and walked around but on the way to hospital he died. He had fractured a rib and it went through the aorta on the journey. The mother was inconsolable. Father Ermelindo spent about a good hour with her. She didn't go home happy or anything but she was relieved.

That Thursday evening we headed to Manorhamilton for the next Mass. That was the smallest crowd but it was the smallest population. There were about 350 people there. Again he talked and it was about eleven o'clock before we got back from there. He did interviews. He did blessings for sick kids. He was so obliging. I was wrecked at this stage. On Friday morning he went to a local hostel with a lot of psychiatric patients and did the Mass there. After that we took him for a drive around Lough Allen and Arigna. He was tired and went to bed. But we then got a call from a lady from a home in Boyle who said she had 60 people who were going to miss him and they were almost all bedridden. I told him and he said, 'If you take me, we'll go.' And so he did. He spent up to two hours with them.

We then drove to Knock and that was the end of it. That was the Padre Pio weekend in September. We handed him back to Eileen Maguire. After that he did the weekend in Knock and then went on for a week in Galway. He then proceeded to the United States. He phoned us afterwards and thanked us. But the loveliest thing happened about a week before that Christmas. I got a call from a delivery company. They had tried to deliver a package and there was nobody in the house. I caught up with them. The parcel contained a box of sweets from Father Ermelindo, from San Giovanni. It was lovely; it wasn't the value, it was just the thought. I couldn't describe the man; he was so simple, so holy and so tolerant. His visit had a tremendous impact on people. They appreciated meeting him so much.

EILEEN MAGUIRE DESCRIBES HOW, FOR MANY DECADES, IRISH DEVOTEES HAVE TRAVELLED IN LARGE NUMBERS TO SAN GIOVANNI ROTONDO.

The pilgrimages grew every year in the 1970s and '80s. The facilities were improving. We would have taken out two groups every year and Mairead Doyle would have taken out two or three groups every year. Gradually, interest increased. People eventually visited Rome, Assisi and San Giovanni as part of the tour. Every year we would add one of the other areas. But the one constant has always been San Giovanni Rotondo.

All types go, rich and poor. We have people who can't handle the Italian heat and who get upset. Invariably, once they reach San Giovanni they calm down. There is always great kindness and a wonderful spirit. If a little old lady can't manage her bag the men will carry it. They are helped all along the way by the group. Many can't get there independently; they have to be part of a group. They meet every evening and share their experiences. There always is a lovely feeling.

There are many, many people who have worries. If you have a worry you will turn to somebody. So many people turn to Padre Pio in a time of need. In my groups I have people who are very ill or people praying for someone very ill. There is always a reason why someone wants to go to San Giovanni. There are always people who are hurting. Once they become hooked they go back again and again. Some even go for a week every year. It is something they feel they have to do.

GEMMA DILLON, COUNTY MEATH, HELPED ORGANISE
THE FIRST FULL PLANE-LOAD OF IRISH PILGRIMS TO SAN
GIOVANNI. THEY TRAVELLED FOR THE VISIT OF POPE JOHN
PAUL II ON 25 MAY 1987, MARKING THE CENTENARY OF PADRE
PIO'S BIRTH.

The plane was full of Padre Pio pilgrims travelling to mark
the centenary. There were three groups, one organised
around Derry by Sean Mulrine, another organised by Eileen
Maguire through the Padre Pio office in Dublin, and the third
organised by myself around Meath, Westmeath and Cavan. I
suppose 150 or 160 travelled in all, with each of us allocated
a certain number of seats. My seats were snapped up on the
first day and I had a waiting-list of 80. We could have filled
an Airbus.

The trip left on 21 May. Before we took off we were all so
proud that we had photographs taken under the fuselage of
the plane. It was a week-long trip. Because of the importance
of the occasion we were permitted to fly into Bari Airport,
which wasn't too far from San Giovanni. My group headed to
Pietrelcina because it was quite close. We spent two days there
and we were actually there for the birthday of Padre Pio. The
other two groups went directly to San Giovanni. We followed
them there from Pietrelcina.

Our group arrived in San Giovanni at around seven o'clock
in the evening. The town was crowded in anticipation of the
Pope's visit the next day. It reminded me of the Pope's visit
to Ireland where everybody was walking up and down the
streets and there was an atmosphere of celebration. We sat
on our hotel balcony and watched the preparations for the
Pope's visit taking place down below.

The Pope said Mass in the early afternoon of the next day
in what I think was the football field. If you stood up at the
top of San Giovanni you could actually see down to where the
Mass was being celebrated because it was a good deal lower
and they hadn't got all the high-rise hotels at the time. We

were all in small sections. Our group was together, slightly to the right. We squeezed our way up, which was typical of the determination of the Irish. We had a good view.

The Pope came in a popemobile through the crowd onto the platform. He stood on the altar they had erected on the field. The excitement was incredible but it was an easily managed crowd because everybody was there for the one reason. Everyone was courteous and kind. The weather was lovely; there was lots of sunshine and it was warm. A stained-glass panel depicting Padre Pio looking down on Knock was presented on behalf of the Irish group. We almost had palpitations being in the presence of the Pope saying Mass for Padre Pio.

The Pope was there for most of that afternoon. He blessed pilgrims and I think he drove around. Then he went back up to the monastery and he spent that evening with the friars. He also visited the tomb of Padre Pio. He stayed in the hospital, the Home for the Relief of Suffering, until the next morning and then returned to Rome.

The visit of the Pope meant a lot to us. Many felt that Padre Pio had been marginally sidelined by the Church. He was never fully accepted. The fact that the Pope attended that Mass was like a seal of approval. It was very special for our group to be present. We came back feeling that we were on the right track and approved of.

DEVOTEE PATRICIA COMISKEY, NEWRY, WITH A STORY FROM HER TRIP TO SAN GIOVANNI IN JUNE 2005.
There is this convent in San Giovanni Rotondo. We were looking for directions and we rang the doorbell. We didn't even know it was a convent because the name was written in Italian. We met this wee nun who helped us. Then, the night before we left we decided to go down to see the nuns. The nun we had met said, 'Wait until you see what we have.' She brought us into this toilet. The two of us looked at this toilet

and thought, 'What are we supposed to be looking at here?' It was just a wee toilet with a wash-basin. She said, 'Do you sense anything?' I said, 'No, I don't sense anything here.'

Anyway, this wee nun started telling us this story. She said that they were all out at Mass and got locked out of the convent. That was a big sin for them to get locked out of the convent in the middle of January. They were all freezing. It was desperate regarding how they were going to get in. They were wondering what they were going to do. It was really freezing cold. The Mother Superior said, 'Padre Pio will look after us, he'll let us in.'

They got the caretaker. He came and said the only way he could do it was to break the toilet window, which he did. He got in. The man said that they should all go into the kitchen to get warmed up. It was cold and they could all feel the cold air hitting them. He said that he would go and clean up all the glass and mud because it was quite mucky, and he would board up the window for them.

He went and got the brush and the shovel. As he was about to go through the toilet door, he got this blast that blinded him. It stopped him in his tracks. When the flash cleared and he got his sight back again, he looked and the window was totally formed. A new pane of glass was there, there was no muck on the toilet seat or on the floor. All the glass that he had shattered had gone and the window was perfect.

He couldn't believe it. He called all the nuns and they couldn't believe it. But the Mother Superior said, 'I told you Padre Pio would look after us.' They have taken the broken pane of glass and they've put it in a frame up on a wall in the convent. And they just have ordinary glass now back in the toilet. The wee nun, who is Filipino, and I have remained friends ever since. We talk on the phone frequently from Ireland to San Giovanni.

STELLA ENRIGHT (NÉE MacSWEENEY), COUNTY KERRY, REMEMBERS HER PILGRIMAGE TO PIETRELCINA, PADRE PIO'S BIRTHPLACE, IN THE LATE 1970s.

Pietrelcina was a very poor place, all the houses were very old and it was full of hills. You went up this little narrow street, up a hill, and you had stone houses with small windows and a door. You went in one door and it was a kitchen where you had the bench where he used to sit. You came down the street and there was a flight of steps which you went up. It brought you into this little room where his bed was.

I remember walking in and I looked at the bed. On it I saw a kind of drawing of the head and shoulders of Padre Pio. It was like a bust of him. I thought to myself, 'When I come out will I say anything or not?' When I came down someone said to me, 'Did you see anything?' I said, 'I did.' Then, everyone said they saw something too. More people saw what I saw and others saw him on the cross.

When I was in the kitchen I was walking around with the group. The bench was kind of covered with thick Cellophane paper, like you would use for silage. It was covered like that; nowadays it is all glassed in. I rubbed my hand along the bench. There must have been a little hole in the Cellophane and when I took away my hand there was this tiny piece of the wood in my hand. I still have that.

Pietrelcina was nice and it was where he lived. But San Giovanni is more uplifting. The atmosphere is magical, you can sense it. You can sense his spirit around there. It's more spiritually uplifting than Pietrelcina.

PATRICIA COMISKEY RECALLS ANOTHER OCCURRENCE FROM HER TRIP TO SAN GIOVANNI IN 2005.

We stayed in this house owned by an old woman who had her hair tied back. We were given a room in the basement and there was nobody else about but us. On the second morning I paid her and she was over the moon. She put her arms around me and thanked me. She indicated to us that she wanted us to go down the corridor with her. She opened this locked door and brought us in.

Well, you never saw a room like it. It was a beautiful room, blue and bright inside. She had all these artefacts of Padre Pio. She had slippers and she had vests belonging to him. She opened this wardrobe and she allowed us to touch the things we wanted to touch. There were shoes, she had Rosary beads belonging to him and I think she had one of his mittens. The next thing was she locked up all the things again and she brought us into another room.

The other room was full of pictures. She started going on in Italian. There were pictures of people I presumed must have been her parents. I don't know who they were. Then she came to this picture, a real old picture, and I presumed it was her. It looked to be her on her Holy Communion day and Padre Pio had his hands on her shoulders. She must have been quite important because there were photographs of her with all the priests in San Giovanni. She was always dressed in her best regalia outside the Basilica and the priests were surrounding her.

We thought she was a relation or a niece of Padre Pio's, that's what we felt. We decided to ask a nun we had met. I asked, 'Who is that lady we stayed with?' All she said was, 'She is a spiritual child of Padre Pio.' I had never heard of a spiritual child of Padre Pio but I gather they do exist. She then said, 'Have you not heard that Padre Pio said he would never rest until all the spiritual children were in heaven?' or something like that. That was all she said. It left me with my eyes open going, 'What?' Obviously, Padre Pio could see through her and that she would carry on his life; that she wouldn't let him down. She was a very special, holy woman.

EILEEN REA ON HER PILGRIMAGES TO PADRE PIO'S TOMB AT
SAN GIOVANNI ROTONDO AND TO PIETRELCINA.

The first time I went to visit the tomb, everyone that asked me
to pray for them flashed through my mind. Way back in 1982,
when I first went out there, we had the most wonderful times
compared with today. There weren't the crowds that are going
today. We were able to spend a lot more time at the tomb. You
wouldn't feel that you were taking up a space that somebody
else wanted. We went down to Pietrelcina where he was born.
We put our heads on the stone that he lay down on and we sat
on the chair. But now they are all covered completely with a
very thick glass to preserve them because people were taking
little chips away.

The feeling I get in San Giovanni is absolutely tremendous.
You feel Our Lady's presence in a big way, especially up in
his cell where he died and where he spent his nights in his
little room. You feel this warm glow. You have this closeness.
You feel that somebody has their arms around you. There's
such a deep presence. It's so hard to explain it. It's absolutely
wonderful. I keep thinking to myself, 'If this is like heaven it
would be a wonderful place to go to.'

PATRICIA COMISKEY ALSO RECALLS HER VISIT TO PADRE PIO'S
TOMB.

We were there during the week, when it's not so busy. They
let you go down and you can kneel beside his tomb at night.
They open up the gates after the Rosary. You can actually go
in and touch his tomb and say a few prayers. Because there's
only a very small crowd it's very, very quiet and just lovely.
It's much better than during the day when there are maybe
100 people there and they are all sitting around and it's not
as quiet as it should be. At night there were only about two
dozen of us. They all seemed to be fairly local. The woman
beside me started to cry. She was only a young mother. She was
Italian, she couldn't speak English and I couldn't speak Italian.

I thought, 'She's here obviously because there's somebody she's praying for too.' I left then. I felt a lovely serenity. I really did.

STELLA ENRIGHT (NÉE MacSWEENEY) EXPLAINS HOW, FOR CLOSE TO A DECADE FROM THE MID-1970s TO THE MID-1980s, SHE DID VOLUNTARY WORK IN SAN GIOVANNI DURING HER HOLIDAYS.

Around 1970 I met Father Alessio when he came to Listowel. He was the priest who looked after Padre Pio for the last years of his life. A few of us, who had devotion to Padre Pio, got together and printed posters and got things going. He came back regularly and we became the best of friends. Through that friendship I decided, during the first year I was working, to go out to San Giovanni to help out.

I was able to type so I spent many hours each day in the office doing the Irish correspondence for Father Alessio. I put Mass card acknowledgements into envelopes and posted them to names and addresses that were on forms I was given. The cards had a picture of Our Lady of Grace on them. You would put in with the cards one of the Padre Pio prayer leaflets. I used to know the names and addresses, the town names and the townlands. Every county in Ireland was covered. There was a wealth of stuff coming in from all over the country.

Every year, for the next nine or ten years until I got married, I used to go out there. I would give one week to them each year. It was all voluntary work. I loved it. It wasn't so commercialised at the time. I even got to know the locals in the shops. I used to love the day I arrived in San Giovanni. I felt as if Padre Pio was welcoming me home. The day I was leaving I'd be heartbroken.

DEATH AND BEYOND

AT HALF PAST TWO ON THE MORNING OF 23
September 1968, Padre Pio died at the Capuchin friary at
San Giovanni Rotondo. Bus-loads of mourners immediately
arrived to pay their respects. The Irish were in attendance.
Some arrived singly, or in small groups, in the aftermath of his
death. Others, such as Kay Thornton from County Dublin,
had been returning from a pilgrimage to San Giovanni when
the tragic news broke. Retracing her steps from Rome, she
joined the chaotic mass of humanity that had congregated
back in San Giovanni to view Padre Pio's remains.

Until noon on 26 September the corpse remained on public
view. Then, in beautiful sunshine and in the presence of
100,000 mourners, the casket containing the body of Padre
Pio was placed in an open hearse and carried slowly from
the church through the town of San Giovanni Rotondo. The
journey, encompassing a round trip of little more than three
miles, took in excess of three hours. At ten o'clock that evening
the coffin of Padre Pio was placed in a crypt.

International pressure instantaneously arose for the
beatification of Padre Pio. That pressure was also manifest
in Ireland where devotion to the friar had grown rapidly,
encouraged by the expansion of prayer groups and access to
his relics. Pilgrims from all parts of the country travelled to

Italy each year. News of his intercessions, miracles and cures was sent from Ireland, north and south, to the Capuchins at San Giovanni Rotondo. Soon, his Irish supporters were clamouring for Padre Pio's elevation to sainthood.

The diocesan process for the cause of Padre Pio's beatification and canonisation opened in San Giovanni Rotondo in 1983. In 1990, with an Irish delegation in attendance, the process was formally brought to an end. Close to 4,000 Irish people attended the beatification on 2 May 1999. Some 4,000 returned for the canonisation on 16 June 2002. With representatives from Ireland playing formal roles on both occasions, the final elevation of Padre Pio to the pantheon of saints thus came to a close.

KAY THORNTON, COUNTY DUBLIN, WHO VISITED SAN GIOVANNI DURING THE WEEK OF PADRE PIO'S DEATH, WAS ONE OF THE LAST IRISH PEOPLE TO SEE HIM ALIVE. SHE ALSO ATTENDED HIS FUNERAL.

My sister wanted to see Padre Pio before he died. We went out the week of his death although there was no talk of him dying at the time. We were at his Mass first and we were received by him and we got his blessing. He was very old and very frail. He was hardly able to move. He had to be helped onto the altar. He was sitting down during the Mass. He stumbled on the way back into the vestry and someone had to catch him.

We had just left San Giovanni when we heard of Padre Pio's death. We came back from Rome overnight on the train and we were there for the funeral. I was determined to go back although most people stayed in Rome. I kissed him laid out in the coffin. It was unbelievable how many people were there. You couldn't move with the people. People were queuing night and day to pass the coffin. There were so many coming, and the doors had to be closed for the funeral. The people nearly went crazy because they couldn't get in. It was very moving. It was very special to have been there.

HUBERT Mc HUGH, COUNTY LEITRIM, SAW THE FUNERAL OF
PADRE PIO ON AN OLD BLACK AND WHITE TELEVISION SET
IN ATHLONE.

I was in boarding school in Athlone in 1968. There wasn't
much television at that time in boarding school, nor were
there many televisions back in Leitrim either. But they did let
us see the news the evening of Padre Pio's funeral. We were
all at study and nothing ever interrupted it. For the news that
particular evening we were all brought out of study. We didn't
know what was wrong. I had never heard of Padre Pio at the
time. But they were Marist Brothers and they wanted us to
see it.

There were two study rooms, one was up to third year and
then there was fourth and fifth year. We were the young guys
in the junior study. We were brought over to this smaller study
where the fourth and fifth years would be. We wouldn't have
got newspapers at that time but they would have left one or
two for the fourth and fifth years. There was a television in
that study. To us it was like crossing the great divide to get in
there. The fourth and fifth years were like gods, as if they had
got it all.

What they were showing on the news was Padre Pio's funeral
in San Giovanni in black and white. There were huge crowds.
This big square was black with people. There were thousands
milling there. When I went to San Giovanni later, it was one
of the things I wanted to see. There were loads of monks and
priests, the celebration of the Mass and a big casket. There
was the old church as well. They also showed some pictures
of Padre Pio waving from a window and little bits of paper
flying. I think that was his last appearance at the window.

To us it was an amazing thing to be brought out of the study
to watch the news. We only saw a few programmes, *Buntús
Cainte*, *Labhair Gaeilge Linn* and *The Riordans* on a Sunday
night. It never deviated from that. So this was quite a big
event. It meant so much to be brought across to see it. They

then gave us a little talk. They told us about the stigmata, which I didn't understand. They told us about some religious books that we could read. After that I read a wee bit about him.

It certainly had a huge bearing on me. It was something very similar to the assassination of President John F. Kennedy. At that time we had only the old wet-and-dry-battery radio. But Padre Pio's death stuck with me more, maybe because of the television pictures. Also, Italy was so distant to me back then. That night certainly has stuck with me ever since.

GEMMA DILLON, COUNTY MEATH, DESCRIBES THE OPENING AT SAN GIOVANNI, IN MARCH 1983, OF THE DIOCESAN PROCESS FOR THE CAUSE OF PADRE PIO'S BEATIFICATION AND CANONISATION. EIGHT CARDINALS, 31 ARCHBISHOPS AND 72 BISHOPS ATTENDED ALONG WITH 20,000 DEVOTEES. There was an open-air Mass and some Irish group leaders, about eight or nine of us, were invited to come to San Giovanni to take part. We arrived just after midnight on the Saturday and we were at the square in front of the Basilica at eight o'clock on the Sunday morning. There weren't many Irish there, it was mostly Italian. I was delighted to be among them.

The previous evening the Archbishop had decided to hold the ceremony out of doors to accommodate the crowd. They had erected an altar outside the main doors of the Basilica. We all arrived full of excitement. The ceremony was scheduled to commence at ten o'clock but everything started over an hour later. Some people were dressed in extraordinary finery, flowing chiffon, lovely hats and gowns. I had this warm, woolly suit on and a hat that was quite comfortable and warm.

Mass started, with some of it in Italian and the readings in English. Just before the Offertory the thunder clapped, the lightning flared and the rain came down in torrents. It was coming down in bucket loads. Everyone in their finery was absolutely soaked. They had to run for cover and couldn't appear in public again for the rest of that afternoon. Some of their gowns stuck to them.

After half an hour of this torrential rain, the priests gathered up all the bits and they moved the Mass inside the Basilica. The whole thing was suspended in time while everybody moved in. I was shooed in because I had gifts to present and I was put in a nice vantage point. I had been asked to present something on behalf of my prayer group in Navan, so I presented Waterford Crystal bud vases, one on behalf of the prayer group and the other on behalf of my husband Eddie and myself.

The ceremony concluded with many important documents being read and signed by those appointed to investigate the cause. I remember all these books being brought out and placed on the altar after Mass. I felt I was part of something very sacred and historic. Afterwards, Father Alessio referred to the finery that had been ruined by the rain and said to the group, 'That will teach you not to be so vain.' Padre Pio had obviously taken one look at all the glamour and finery and decided to bring it all into line with his own simple way of life.

SEAN MULRINE, DERRY, REMEMBERS THE PIVOTAL DAY IN 1990 WHEN THE DOCUMENTATION CONTAINING THE WRITINGS OF PADRE PIO, EVIDENCE OF GRACES AND CURES RECEIVED AND OTHER RELEVANT DOCUMENTS WERE FORMALLY HANDED OVER AT SAN GIOVANNI FOR CONSIDERATION BY ROME. THE CONCLUSIONS OF AN ECCLESIASTICAL TRIBUNAL, WHICH INTERVIEWED 73 PEOPLE IN 182 SESSIONS, WERE PRESENTED. A FURTHER 10,000 PAGES OF WRITINGS BY AND ABOUT PADRE PIO WERE SUBMITTED BY A HISTORICAL COMMISSION. THE PROCESS SUBSEQUENTLY CULMINATED IN THE BEATIFICATION AND CANONISATION OF PADRE PIO.

We were invited to San Giovanni when they did all the books and took them away for the cause of the beatification of Padre Pio. The Papal Nuncio came up from Rome and the Archbishop was there. It was in Our Lady of Grace church in San Giovanni. Ann and I were invited to it and we had seats on the altar. Mairead Doyle, the Padre Pio devotee from Dublin, was sitting beside me at that service.

That was the service for the start of the beatification process. All the books, all the dates, were taken away by the Archbishop and the head man for the cause. They were all stamped and sealed on the altar and put in big crates and taken away to the Vatican for examination so that things could go forward for the beatification of Padre Pio.

The church was packed and the street was packed. There were dozens and dozens of bishops. The atmosphere was electric. It was fabulous. So many dignitaries were there. Senator Des Hanafin and his wife Mona were there from Ireland. Franco Zeffirelli, the film producer, was there as well. I don't know what Padre Pio would have thought of it. All he ever wanted to be was a humble priest that liked to pray. But it was a great event.

NUALA BRADY, FORMER ITALIAN PILGRIMAGE MANAGER FOR JOE WALSH TOURS, HELPED ORGANISE THE BEATIFICATION AND CANONISATION TRIPS IN 1999 AND 2002 RESPECTIVELY.

It was a huge campaign to get the people out there. There was a lot of planning and organisation that had to go into it because it took time to get the hotels. At ten o'clock at night we'd still be working getting beds and things like that. We tried to get into every hotel we could think of. We rolled it out to make sure they all got the e-mails and we'd be first in there with our requests. Because our name was so good in Rome and San Giovanni, after all our years there, I must say we were well looked after. The beatification was bigger. Some people didn't go again because they had been to one. We had larger aircraft, and we staggered them. We also went into Bari as well, and into Rome. It all seemed to work out although at the time I was probably tearing my hair out. They all loved it and I really enjoyed it.

EILEEN MAGUIRE, DIRECTOR OF THE IRISH OFFICE FOR PADRE PIO, DUBLIN, ATTENDED THE BEATIFICATION IN 1999.

Immediately the beatification was announced, people started organising groups and trips. In typically Italian style, tickets weren't produced until the very last moment. I flew over to collect tickets for the Irish. They tried to involve all the countries that had been loyal and devoted. We got over 2,000 tickets and we distributed them as fairly as we could to all the groups that were travelling. Finally, I handed the balance of my tickets into the Irish College because they were looking for some more tickets too.

Rome came to a standstill. It was unbelievable. St Peter's filled up by six o'clock in the morning. People parked outside. There was a sort of a park-and-ride system but it left you a distance from the Vatican. Then you had to walk. Everybody was walking on foot because the buses weren't allowed to approach the key areas. The people were crowding into the square from all over the world. There were flags from everywhere. The square was completely full.

I stayed just beside the Vatican because I was taking part in the ceremony and had to take my place at a specific time. I did one of the readings before the actual ceremony began. It was in Irish and it was put in as a tribute to the Irish. They had some readings from his letters and some readings in different languages. Just to look down that square and to see everybody, the sea of people, was amazing. There wasn't a space in the whole square. The feeling was that you were part of this very special ceremony.

St Peter's was completely covered in scaffolding. They were washing the front of it. But on the front of the scaffolding was this banner which was completely covered up. We might have had difficulty following things because the Mass was in Italian. But, when it came to the beatification, once the covering on the banner began to be unfurled there was no problem. Everybody looked up at the façade as a picture of Padre Pio was slowly uncovered. You heard clapping. Everybody began to cheer. There were tears. It was awesome.

After the beatification there was a reception. An enormous cake was wheeled in. It was almost like a birthday cake. All the Italian friars from San Giovanni Rotondo stood around this cake. They were crying. They were clapping and clapping. The joy was palpable. There were fireworks that night and the whole sky of Rome was lit up. Everybody just stood and cheered.

We knew he was glorified in heaven but now he was glorified on earth as well. Everybody had prayed for this. There we were in Rome and this was it, this was the glorification of the man. This was the moment that we had prayed for, for so long. Father Alessio always said, 'He deserved that, for his life of holiness, for his life of suffering, for his life of inspiration to everybody.' The beatification was a very special moment.

ASSUMPTA O'BRIEN, COUNTY KILDARE, TRAVELLED FOR THE CANONISATION IN 2002.
I was out there with a contingent from Dublin. We got up very early on the morning of the canonisation. We had breakfast about five o'clock. We walked to St Peter's Square for about seven o'clock even though Mass was at ten. We were there trying to find our seats. Everybody just found their seats, grabbed them and sat down. There were flags from every nation displayed with pride. There were Irish flags and banners there. All the different prayer groups from Ireland had their own banners saying where they were from. They even had T-shirts saying where they were from and what prayer group they belonged to.

It was a very, very hot day. The temperature was in excess of 30 degrees. The place was crammed; there were more than 500,000 people at the event, young, old and infirm. Head cover was essential. The local council provided us with water. They had trucks everywhere, handing out bottles of water to everybody. Nobody had to pay for it. It mightn't have been holy water but it was a blessed relief to our parched throats!

Around a quarter to ten the Pope arrived. I could see him clearly enough. He was quite feeble at the time and required a bit of assistance. He spoke mostly in Italian. We sat entranced, doing our best to concentrate and pray. We had our eyes and ears open so that we wouldn't miss a syllable of what he was trying to say. Mentally he was as sharp as ever. What I remember most was when he uttered Padre Pio's name, making him a saint, it was acclaimed with ecstatic reverence. There was a phenomenal cheer and lots of clapping.

People were very emotional, people were praying and crying. People had been praying for so long for him to be made a saint. He was also a man we could all relate to, he had lived in our own lifetime. Some had been to Confession with him; a number had met him in the flesh. Suddenly, here was our prayer being answered. This was the ultimate, it was the big moment.

Everybody had their reason for being there. There were 500,000 reasons, for sure. Some were in thanksgiving; others were still doing novenas for something. Personally, mine was in thanksgiving. I would have attributed many things that happened in my life to him. I had major surgery on my throat and at the end of the surgery the results came back clear. My consultant asked me, 'Can I ask you who you prayed to?' Even with my children he has helped with different things that happened in their lives. He is the one person that they would pray to. I also have a first-class relic which I have given to people and some have claimed to have been cured.

To me, personally, the canonisation meant a lot. The first I had heard of Padre Pio was from my father. I used to hear him talking about the monk in Italy who had the stigmata. I was 14 or 15 at the time. Then, Padre Pio passed away in September 1968 and I remember seeing the funeral on black and white television. It was in our living-room. My father was glued to it. He was very upset. I can remember seeing these throngs of people behind the coffin. I can still see that picture in my mind, of people squashed together. At a later stage, after my father had passed on, Padre Pio started to come back into my life. And once he comes into your life he doesn't really leave it.

After the canonisation we went back to our hotel. We watched the Spain versus Ireland match in the World Cup. That night in St Peter's Square the fireworks were amazing. There also was a spectacular concert with the life of Padre Pio being re-enacted. But the fireworks were the most amazing I have ever seen. They lit up the Roman sky. It was just fabulous. It was a wonderful end to a most magnificent day.

I was very proud to be there and to be part of it. Little did I ever imagine when I was young that I would one day attend the canonisation of a saint! I felt very much a sense of peace and contentment, there's no question about it. I go back every year since then to San Giovanni. I just go on my own on a flight to Rome and take the train and go up. For me it is the most peaceful place on earth. It is the only place where I feel totally at peace and contented.

EILEEN MAGUIRE ALSO ATTENDED THE CANONISATION.
I was invited to do the reading during the Mass. During the beatification the reading was done by an American lady but it was great to think that we were invited to do the English reading during the canonisation. I was pleased for the Irish. I felt I was representing everybody in Ireland. There was a different picture used for the canonisation; the one of his hand up in blessing was used. This was the banner that was hanging up. St Peter's was finished and the façade was beautiful.

While the canonisation was just as lovely as the beatification, there was almost a sense of déjà vu. We had been there. There was also a tinge of sadness to the event because two men who had been so involved had died at the beginning of 2000 within three months of one another. They were Father Alessio and Father Joseph Pius. I felt their absence badly, as did many people. They were missed, yet I felt, 'They are here.'

It really was extremely hot. The heat was unbelievable. People were dropping like flies. Even a cardinal passed out beside me. The wife of a member of the government got weak. They were wheeling people out all the time. They were even spraying the crowd with a water cannon to keep people cool. Although the Holy Father was alert, he wasn't well. His will must have been of steel to take that whole event.

There must have been up to 4,000 people who travelled out from all over Ireland. Nobody could get accommodation in Rome. They were staying outside Rome, getting up at two o'clock and three o'clock in the morning and travelling into Rome. Yet there was no word of complaint, everybody was happy. I had been at every event: the opening of the process, the closing of the process, the submission of everything to Rome and then the beatification and the canonisation. It was extraordinary that all of that had taken place in my lifetime.

FATHER MICHAEL DUGGAN RECALLS THE DEATH OF MAIREAD DOYLE, FOUNDER OF THE FIRST PADRE PIO PRAYER GROUP IN IRELAND, WHO KNEW PADRE PIO PERSONALLY AND WHO DIED IN SAN GIOVANNI JUST DAYS AFTER ATTENDING THE CANONISATION CEREMONY.

In June 2002 we were out in Rome for the canonisation of Padre Pio. Mairead wasn't well at that time. She had been ill for some time before. But she did take part in the ceremonies. She brought up a gift to the late Holy Father during the ceremony. Three days after that we went down to San Giovanni. It's about a three-hour or four-hour drive from Rome. The group that she was with were down at his tomb one night. I had gone on my own to the tomb. I then came down to the hotel quite tired after all the ceremonies and I went to bed.

At about quarter to ten I heard shouting on the corridor. I woke up from my sleep and I thought it was a baby. I came out to find Mairead at the door of her room saying, 'I'm dying, I want help.' I put her into bed and got her a drink of water. Her sisters were having tea downstairs, nobody had heard her. I said, 'Go up immediately and I'll try and get a doctor.' She was quite ill. As I was trying to get the doctor, a friend of the family came down and said, 'Father, you'd better come up. She's not well. We think she's going.' I had the holy oils, I went up, prayed over her, gave her absolution and anointed her. She opened her eyes twice and died.

She had travelled well over 100 times to San Giovanni with groups. She knew Padre Pio personally and her family had met him. She was a real devotee and she died in San Giovanni. So we had Mass for her there in San Giovanni, in the hospital. The remains didn't come back home until about a week later. She was brought to her own parish church in East Wall. Cardinal Connell was there at the reception of the remains the evening before. We then had a concelebrated Mass, with about 16 or 17 priests, on the morning of her funeral.

She used to say that Padre Pio said that he'd always welcome his children into heaven. She believed that and I would say, in hindsight, it would be the place where she would have liked to have died. So, while the shock was great to her sisters, in hindsight, as time went on, they came around to seeing it as a grace that he took her home where she first met him.

MARY BRIODY, NIECE OF MAIREAD DOYLE, CONTINUES THE STORY OF HER DEATH.
I was with her and I shared a room with her on that trip. She was old at the time, just a month short of her eightieth birthday. Even the walk up with the gift to the Pope at the canonisation in Rome was a tremendous trek for her, but she was determined. She knelt down and was sort of chatting to the Pope. I was amused. I said to her, 'What did you say to the Pope?' She told me she said, 'Holy Father, my first thought of the day is for you and I pray for you every day.' He said, 'I'll pray for you.'

That night she said to me, 'Now, what will I do?' She was so happy. It was the culmination of her life's work. She was thrilled and so delighted that she had lived to see it. All along, when she'd go out there she'd ask, 'Any word about his canonisation?' The minute she found out she was all excited. She got wind of it before it was public knowledge. Then, when it happened she said, 'It's all done now.' I said, 'Sure, you'll continue to bring more pilgrims to San Giovanni.' Years before, she had said to me, 'You'll live to see him as a saint, I mightn't, make sure to go.' I said, 'I will.' She used to always say on the bus, 'If anything happens to me, my niece will continue to go.' But she did live to see it. She was really, really happy. And I do continue to go.

We went to San Giovanni on the next day. She went up to the tomb where there was a Rosary going on. She came back to the hotel and she wasn't feeling well. We didn't think there was going to be anything wrong. She got a cup of tea and she was very hot so we got a fan. I normally went for a walk so she said, 'Are you going for your walk?' I said, 'No, I'm only going down for a cup of tea, I'll be up in a few minutes.' She must have felt unwell because she called Father Duggan. He didn't think she was going to die because he came down and said, 'Mairead is not well,' but he didn't think there was any danger. Yet the minute I walked into the room, I knew.

It was terrible for us at the time. But, looking back, it was the best thing that could have happened. She kind of had two funerals then. All the friars came out to her funeral and the Bishop came. They put notices up around San Giovanni to say about all the work she did for Padre Pio. In Italy they put these paper notices up all around. They were in Italian with a bit in English near the end. I still have one. It was lovely. It was a glorious end after her lifetime of work. Her full work was devoted to making Padre Pio a saint.

FOLLOWING HIS CANONISATION IN 2002, PADRE PIO BECAME IRELAND'S MOST POPULAR SAINT, TOPPING POLLS OF FAVOURITE INTERCESSORS AND ATTAINING ICONIC STATUS THROUGHOUT THE ISLAND. AFTER ALMOST HALF A CENTURY OF DEVOTION HIS POPULARITY WAS UNPRECEDENTED, ACCORDING TO FATHER JACK Mc ARDLE SS.CC.

He obviously filled a vacuum and there must have been a need or he would never have received the response he got. Irish religion was rather drab and unexciting at the time Padre Pio came on the scene. Religion was about the missions, hellfire and brimstone. We didn't have any miracles and we weren't expecting any. We then heard about this holy man who could do so many things. Here was a man with special powers and people got healed. The Irish were very open to that.

His credibility was there, whether people saw it or not. He had to be all that he was or there wouldn't have been any response at all. He had to be the real thing, that he really did have a hotline to God. All that had to be established long before people ever heard of him. People going out to San Giovanni even today will talk about the atmosphere or the sense of presence. Otherwise, nothing would have happened, it would have all been stillborn.

He was also very hard on himself. His whole life was a sort of pilgrimage to Lough Derg or Croagh Patrick. The Irish could relate to that. It wouldn't be an Italian thing; they are not into suffering too much. There was that dimension as well, where suffering was always seen as part of the package.

The timing of Father Alessio in coming over to Ireland and telling people who wouldn't have known about him was vital. There was a massive blitz and many significant people emerged, from Eileen Maguire to Mona Hanafin and Sean Mulrine. They travelled the country and they got the response. There was a need there that they met. There was a hunger in the Irish people.

As a result, he joined Pope John XXIII, President John F.

Kennedy and de Valera on the walls of Irish houses. A priest friend of mine says he can walk into a hospital ward and look around and he knows the Catholics because they all have something of Padre Pio on their beds or on their lockers. His stickers are on cars. It's really quite extraordinary.

FATHER PIUS McLAUGHLIN OFM PRESENTS HIS FINAL ASSESSMENT OF PADRE PIO.

He was a simple Capuchin who spent his life saying Mass and hearing Confessions. That was him. That was his spirituality. That was what he was about, those two sacraments, bringing people to God and God to people. And it worked. I really think that God raises up certain people at certain times in history. In our twentieth century, Padre Pio was raised up for a purpose. I think his purpose was to bring relief from a lot of suffering and from the suffering caused by two world wars. He was what I would call a doctor of the soul.

You read about his life and the persecution he suffered, not only from his own Order but from the Church itself, which viewed everything he did, and everything he was, with complete suspicion. If that was being done to me I would say, 'I don't need this,' and that's what most did. But he sat back. He was silenced for a long time, he wasn't allowed to meet with people and there were all kinds of accusations against him. I think his whole life was lived out in obedience to the will of God. Whatever that was going to be, he carried it out. And he had to suffer. But that's why he is a saint.

EILEEN MAGUIRE WITH HER VIEW.

He is human to us. We have pictures of him. We have videos. We even have a video of a day in his life, from morning to evening. We see him walk around and he gets angry with the photographer. So many people saw him and attended his Mass. We have reams of testimony from people who lived with him. They saw his holiness and devotion. We hear of St Thérèse, for example, and many people love her. But they wouldn't have the same access to her as we had to Padre Pio.

He keeps his hand on your back and he shows you the way. I feel he is the sort of person that will push you or point you in a certain direction. He guides people. He always directs people. And he was a humble, holy person. Can you imagine that he never left San Giovanni! He never went looking for funds or money but it came, the letters came piling in. There's a bit of a doubting Thomas in all of us but you can't doubt this man. You can look at him and you can see him and you can see what he has done.

KAY THORNTON OFFERS HER OPINION.

He is one of the most special people of the twentieth century. There was never anyone like him before. He suffered dreadfully all his life. Every single moment of his life he was suffering from those bleeding wounds and they were so sore. He must have been a special person even to survive that.

You never forget Padre Pio. He was a profound man, like nobody I ever met. I am a very lucky person to have met him. He once put his hand on my head and that was the most wonderful thing that ever happened to me. He lets you know when you are not pleasing him and then he helps you when you do something right. He is always with you, he is always there.

MONA HANAFIN ADDS HER PERSPECTIVE.

Following his death he was such a loss. But he did say that when he died more people would come to San Giovanni than ever did when he was alive. There are eight million going there each year now. They come from every corner of the world, including Ireland, to see him.

His whole life was dedicated to saving souls. He was a tireless confessor. You had St Francis and St Anthony but in our times of trouble you had Padre Pio. He was special, he was just sent to us for our time. And why did he do it? He didn't do it for himself; he did it for us, for mankind.

I always say to people, 'You don't pray to Padre Pio, you pray through him because if the Lord doesn't wish it then it won't happen.' I would hope that, please God, if I ever meet him he will look kindly on me. I definitely regard him as the greatest mystic ever.

GEMMA DILLON'S CONCLUDING WORDS.

I think he has great compassion and great love for those he calls his spiritual children. I have also found him to be a very hard taskmaster. You will never get anything easily by being his disciple or spiritual child. I think he is hard to please. He suffered so greatly and he preached all the time that suffering is never wasted. He said to use it wisely, use it well and get the maximum benefit out of it.

I believe he expects the very best from you in everything that you do. But I always feel that if you hang in there it will be alright. He taught me to tolerate myself, put up with others and to forgive generously. When I meet him, if I ever do, I'll quake in front of him, yet I know he'll be glad to see me. I know he will open his arms and say, 'Come on over here, I'll give you a hug.'